MIDDLE EAST AVENUE

MIDDLE EAST AVENUE

Female Migration from Sri Lanka to the Gulf

Grete Brochmann

Westview Press
BOULDER • SAN FRANCISCO • OXFORD

Published in 1993 in the United States of America by Westview Press, Inc., 5500 Central Avenue, Boulder, Colorado 80301-2877, and in the United Kingdom by Westview Press, 36 Lonsdale Road, Summertown, Oxford OX2 7EW

Library of Congress Cataloging-in-Publication Data
Brochmann, Grete.
Middle East avenue : female migration from Sri Lanka to the Gulf / Grete Brochmann.
p. cm.
Includes bibliographical references and index.
ISBN 0-8133-8617-9
1. Alien labor, Sri Lankan—Persian Gulf Region. 2. Women alien labor—Persian Gulf Region. 3. Women—Sri Lanka. I. Title.
HD8662.B76 1993
331.6'54930536'082—dc20 92-20487
CIP

Printed and bound in the United States of America

The paper used in this publication meets the requirements of the American National Standard for Permanence of Paper for Printed Library Materials Z39.48-1984.

10 9 8 7 6 5 4 3 2 1

Contents

Tables and Figures

Tables

Figures

Preface

The work on this book has been facilitated by generous support from a number of individuals and institutions. I begin with the numerous women whom I interviewed during the fieldwork in Sri Lanka in 1985–1986. These women and their families readily accepted my invasion of their privacy and showed a great deal of tolerance to all my strange questions. I also want to thank the various informants I used in the communities of investigation, who put their comprehensive knowledge about conditions in the areas at my disposal. I particularly want to mention Karuna in the Shanty Canal area, who offered eminent support both as an informant and as a source of inspiration.

I furthermore want to thank research colleagues attached to the Centre for Women's Research (CENWOR), the International Centre for Ethnic Studies (ICES) and the Institute of Sociology at the University of Colombo. Special thanks in this respect go to the Leiden-Colombo Research Team and Programme Director Frank Eelens, who generously opened their voluminous files to me and took part in numerous discussions on research strategies and data interpretation. Officials working with the Norwegian Aid Agency (NORAD) in Colombo, the Planning Unit in the Integrated Rural Development Programme (IRDP) in Hambantota and Redd Barna in Colombo also offered most valuable assistance.

In acknowledging individuals in Norway, I start with my colleague at the Peace Research Institute of Oslo (PRIO), Kumar Rupesinghe, who gave me the idea of developing a research project based on the Middle East migration and subsequently shared his contacts in Sri Lanka with me.

Later in the process my two supervisors, Fredrik Engelstad and Gunnar Sørbø, provided invaluable challenges and stimulation. With their different but complementary approaches, they provided advice in the realms of sociology and development studies.

My husband, Jon Erik Dølvik, has also given substantial advice throughout the process and shared moments of frustration and joy.

I am thankful to each and every one.

Financial support has been provided by the Norwegian Council for Science and the Humanities (NAVF). A three-year full-time scholarship and various travel grants have made the project possible on the material side. Apart from the fieldwork, participation at a number of international seminars and conferences has been financially supported by NAVF. This aid has been most valuable to the project and to the learning process at large.

Last, I want to thank the Peace Research Institute of Oslo, where I have been affiliated for the major part of the project period. Institutional facilities and good colleagues have been highly appreciated. I have spent the last period of writing at the Institute for Social Research (ISF), Oslo, where the facilities have been equally good.

Grete Brochmann
Oslo, Norway

Introduction

In recent decades, the international migration of labour has become increasingly widespread throughout the world. Expanding international trade in labour has developed into a significant feature of the world economy. For many developing countries remittances from citizens temporarily working abroad has become a major source of foreign exchange and has contributed to the reduction of trade deficits.

Alongside the systematic expansion in labour trade, the social issues involved have been increasingly visible. Large numbers of people leave home and family for lengthy stays abroad. Not only is this a dramatic event for the individual, it also affects social relations, culture, the organization of production and consumption patterns in the migrants' local communities.

Basically labour migration is a dynamic social process that can be analyzed on different levels: from the lowest level—the individual actor, the migrant—to the highest—the international society—with numerous gradations in between. The aggregated movements of the individuals involved affect the other levels, and societal structures create and maintain forces that act upon the individual migrant. The interplay of these elements determines the nature and extent of migration.

This book deals with how international macrostructures impinge on the lives of poor people in small communities in a developing country—how the "big world out there" enters remote areas and becomes familiar in an unprecedented way while imposing change in the daily lives of the inhabitants.

Studies of the most common type of international migration—temporary contract circulation—have generally been confined to male migration. A man obtains a short-term work contract in another country, leaving the rest of his family behind. The role of the woman in this context is to maintain the household and perhaps cultivate the land or engage in other economic activities while the man is away. Although women thus form a part of the whole system of migration, they are seldom studied as active participants in it.

In this study I look at a type of labour migration in which the gender component is turned upside down, in which the woman is the main actor who leaves hearth and home in search of work in distant lands. It is the woman who transcends the boundaries of her community, challenging structural and traditional limitations attached to sex and class.

The home country is Sri Lanka, which sends thousands of migrants to work as housemaids in Arab homes in the Gulf area on two-year contracts.[1] The majority of these maids are married; they leave their husbands and children behind in their home communities.

What makes these young women sell their labour power to Arab households, thousands of miles from home, depriving themselves of the possibility of being close to their own children as they grow up? These women have rarely traveled outside their own domain prior to the Gulf move and few have ever traveled by plane. What consequences does this practice have on their lives—as individuals and as members of households, communities and society at large?

The answers to these questions in the broadest sense must be approached on different levels and from different angles. Labour migration must be understood in the context of the economic and social development that has made the migration possible or, rather, has pushed it forward. In other words, the structural dimension of female migration must be outlined in order to explain the position of women in the dynamics of contract labour. The process of labour migration in general is inherently linked to changes in the socioeconomic context in which the moving takes place. Therefore, a comprehensive analysis of causes and consequences of labour migration should approach the phenomenon as a social process in which cultural and political—as well as economic—factors are central.

These contextual factors should be regarded as prerequisites for action—background conditions that make it rational to migrate. We need to search for the relationship between the structural conditions and the motivation of the actors behind the move. Migration should be viewed as a result of both (objective) structural possibilities and/or constraints and human (subjective) appraisals of these factors.

In this book the phenomenon of female labour migration will be analyzed on different levels simultaneously and separately—from the international scene down to the level of the individual woman. It is my aim to reflect and analyze the interaction between the levels—not isolating either the macro structures or the microstructures—in order to see how structural and behavioral preconditions interweave. However, the main focus is on the local communities and the households that the women leave.

Labour migration can also be studied on a wide range of dimensions: Economic, social, cultural, psychological, gender, demographic, political, and so on. Although the focus is on the economic and sociocultural aspects, gender relations will naturally constitute an overriding concern as well. The causes and consequences of female labour migration are likely to be different from those of male migration because women have different social and economic roles in the household and in society at large.

On the causal side the following problems represent the point of departure:

1. Why do the women start migrating? What is their motivation?
2. Do the female migrants constitute a distinctive group as to social class and ethnic group compared to the male migrants? Here we need to study motivation within the frames of social structure: Which factors impel migration in the first place, and which forces maintain the dynamics once it is established?

This question can be related to both the macrolevel (international and national) and the microlevel (communities, households and individuals): Which structural factors induce or necessitate the move, and which motivational factors can contribute to an understanding of individual behaviour?

Along with revealing the possible causes of the phenomenon at the individual, as well as the national/international, level, the consequences of the traffic receive major attention.

The following three sets of problems determine the main direction of the study on the effect side:

1. How do the remittances from abroad affect various levels: the national economy and living conditions in the communities and in individual households? Is the money used in a productive way by the state in the sense that it can have a lasting, positive effect on the economy, or does it create a new dependence on external assets?[2] Do the communities profit from the traffic in terms of new economic activities or increased local demand? Do the households gain substantially in any lasting way?
2. What are the impacts of female migration on social mobility? If upward mobility is taking place, how lasting is the phenomenon when the women stop migrating? What is the impact of migration on patterns of differentiation? Does it reemphasize an already existing mode of differentiation, or does it contribute to levelling out differences? To what extent are the class specific resources of the migrant women influencing their ability to cope with their situations in the Gulf? Are their experiences overseas significantly conditioned by the social status they bear in the first place?
3. On the social and cultural side, how does Middle East migration affect the lives of the women themselves? How are they looked upon by their home community and by society in general? What impact does their experience of a different world have on their environment? How is family life affected—family well-being, division of labour and relations within the household? Is the traffic in any sense a step forward in relation to reduced subordination of the women involved?

Some of these problems, particularly those related to the lives of the women themselves—that is, the questions of reduced subordination and internal relations within the household—are difficult to substantiate. Data are generally scarce, and the field itself has a subtle character. This terrain is nevertheless central to understanding the overall picture and has therefore been included, despite shortcomings in the data, to shed light on an important field within gender studies in developing countries in general, as well as to permit the formulation of hypotheses as to possible consequences in the concrete Sri Lankan context.

Apart from describing and analyzing the specific phenomenon of female labour migration from Sri Lanka to the Middle East, it is the aim of this project to link up with research undertaken in the field of international migration on a theoretical level, particularly research pertaining to Asia. An additional objective is to relate this field of study to the theoretical debate on gender relations in developing societies undergoing the contradictory process of transition to a modern economy.

A major aim of this study, then, is to contribute to a new field of research—female contract-labour migration. It is hoped that the multilevel approach can open up new sets of hypotheses and linkages to stimulate further research.

Many conflicting and contradictory elements are involved in the phenomenon of female labour migration from Sri Lanka. I try to show how individual women act upon these contradictions, both as victims and as beneficiaries of the conditions. Seeming and real contradictions of people's behaviour in relationship to other people and to material structures may give this work direction as a perspective. A multitude of aspects of the phenomenon remain to be fully explored.

Data

Questions related to the time dimension affect all the sets of problems. Ideally the study of economic, sociocultural and gender consequences of labour migration should be done on a longitudinal basis. One should be able to follow the migrants and their communities from the time before the decision was taken to go abroad, through the migration process and subsequently to the situation long after the final return. A study conducted in this way would make possible to appraise the deeper, more lasting effects of the phenomenon.

However, a longitudinal study has not been possible for practical and substantive reasons. For one thing, female labour migration from Sri Lanka is a recent activity, making it de facto impossible to study the long-term effects. Practically speaking, most projects (this one included) do not allow for longitudinal approaches that are time-consuming, expensive and resource-demanding.

Consequently one is confined to synchronous data concerning the actual sample of investigated units. Concerning the past, one has to rely on the memories of the respondents, life histories and material from informants as well as documentation. As to the future, one can propose qualified speculations only.

On an individual project there is also the limitation of having a very small sample of respondents, with the general problems of representativity this entails. To the extent that secondary sources exist, they can help broaden the scope and enrich the field.

This book is a synthesis of secondary sources of various kinds (articles, newspaper clippings, material from donor agencies and development programmes and official documents) and primary data collected during five months of fieldwork in 1985–86 in the slums of Colombo and in the district of Hambantota in southern Sri Lanka.

Some of the secondary data are used to describe and analyze macrostructures—for example, the Sri Lankan political economy and international relations. These quantified data will yield sectional pictures of the macroeconomy and social and political processes in society at large. For reasons of scope it is necessary to cut out certain relevant aspects of the macro structures.

Two national surveys on migrant labour (Korale et al., 1985; Marga, 1986) have been of particular use, since they provide aggregated data on the phenomenon. The first is a report based on three surveys carried out by the Ministry of Plan Implementation, Colombo, in January–October 1984. The three surveys cover structured interviews with (1) 50 licensed recruitment agencies, (2) 900 migrants leaving from the Colombo airport, and (3) a random sample of 424 returned migrants. The report written by the Marga Centre (Sri Lanka Centre for Development Studies) is based on a random sample of 500 returnees. These studies have given a frame of reference to the study presented in this book, which is necessarily based on a much smaller sample.

Generally speaking, secondary data on female migration from Sri Lanka are scarce. The surveys and studies that have been undertaken focus almost exclusively on male migration or gender neutral migration, where figures on women appear only occasionally and where the focus has not been gender oriented. Lack of female-focused data has made this project more difficult but also more challenging.

A research project undertaken by the University of Leiden, the Netherlands, in cooperation with the University of Colombo has been of special relevance, as it has followed some of the same problems as this study and includes some female-specific aspects (Eelens and Speckman, 1990). Cooperating with this research team has been of great value to the project.

The Field: Colombo Slum Pockets and Hambantota

The firsthand data were collected at the microlevel: individual and household interviews and community studies. Individual structured and semistructured interviews were undertaken mainly with migrants who had returned (after one or more contracts), although a few prospective migrants, some nonmigrants and representatives of migrants' families have also been interviewed in a more open manner. The two communities (in a geographically broad sense) were chosen primarily for their dissimilarity in various dimensions—economic basis (urban versus rural/fishing) religion (predominantly Sinhalese versus Muslim) and related cultural differences—to permit a comparison.

Colombo has by far the largest share of the migrant workers to the Middle East, although the total share has been decreasing. In 1981 Colombo sent 50% of the migrants (men and women), whereas the share in 1984 was 35% (Korale et al., 1985). The rest of the migrants are spread fairly evenly throughout the country, with the exception of some higher concentration in certain other cities and urban centres. The great majority of the agencies are located in the city of Colombo, which probably partly explains the predominance of Colombo migrants (85% of all registered agencies in 1981, Korale 1985).

Female migrants are almost invariably recruited from the poorest sections of society. Choosing a major part of the sample in this study from poorer housing areas in Colombo should consequently yield a fairly typical picture.

The various pockets for interviewing were selected with the assistance of persons familiar both with large slum areas of Colombo and, to a certain extent, with the phenomenon of migration (social workers, representatives of nongovernmental organizations [NGOs] and other researchers). One important criterion for selection was the possibility of access to background information on households, living conditions and community life in the areas, as the fieldwork was not of an intensive living-in type.

The bulk of the fieldwork in Colombo was undertaken in a shanty area in the southern part of the city, called Shanty Canal. The Colombo sample is treated as one cluster, although two streets in the north of Colombo (Alutmahawatha and Vestwyke Avenue) will also be handled separately, as these two areas had some interesting special characteristics.

In addition to the 112 systematic interviews with returned migrants, semisystematic and open interviews were carried out with other people living in the areas, including nonmigrant households. Informants of various kinds (local social workers, project officers and researchers, in particular) were also extensively used.

Inside the migrant pockets the households were selected partly with the help of informants (living or working in the area themselves) and partly through a snowball sampling, in which each migrant household indicated another in the neighborhood. The procedure was usually as follows: The informant gave an overview of the area and provided background information on migration as a component of local living conditions. Thereafter he or she gave a list of households that had sent someone to the Gulf. (These lists were complete only in small communities). Often this informant also provided introductions to the first households, which proved a good way of gaining acceptance in the areas. The mission soon became well known to most households, and there were hardly ever any problems of rejection and hostility.

The district of Hambantota is located along the 130-kilometers southern shore of Sri Lanka. The district stretches from the densely populated wet zone in the west far into the dry zone in the east. The population of Hambantota is mainly rural and lives primarily from agriculture, with only 10% living in the towns and urban centres.

The district of Hambantota was chosen as an area for fieldwork for various reasons. Since fieldwork had to be completed within a fairly short period of time, it was important to choose an area where it was easy to get access to secondary data and background information about the communities. It was also of central concern to study a locality that was significantly different from the Colombo sample on important variables to permit a comparison. Hambantota met both requirements. First, Hambantota is a well-documented district, mainly because it is a part of the government's Integrated Rural Development Programme (IRDP), which has made the district the subject of several studies and evaluations. The Norwegian aid agency (NORAD) is the donor in the Hambantota programme, meaning that a fairly large group of Norwegian researchers have been involved in a wide range of studies attached to the IRDP. This fact made it fairly easy to get access to information on different aspects of community life and economic development in the district in advance. Last, through NORAD, contact was facilitated with the District Planning Unit of the IRDP, which is located in the Hambantota township.

Concerning the characteristics of the sample, it was known that a great majority of the migrants were Muslim, rural and semiurban women. It was also known that quite a number of the migrant pockets of the Hambantota township used to live from fishing. These two factors, in addition to the general differences between urban and semiurban/district contexts, constituted an interesting contrast to the Colombo sample as to background variables.

The main sample was chosen from various communities in and around the township of Hambantota, where the migrants were almost invariably Muslim, and where quite a number of the households were living (or used to live) directly or indirectly from fishing. The pockets from which migration was most extensive were identified with assistance from the Planning Unit, and a sample was drawn at random from lists of households provided by the Grama Sevaka (the lowest level of governmental administration in Sri Lanka). It was convenient to use this random sampling (on a modest scale) in Hambantota owing to the high concentration of the migrants, the easy access to the complete lists of inhabitants and the fact that the physical structure of the area was easily overviewed. Since the snowball sampling that was used in the slums of Colombo was not applied in Hambantota, the respondents were not a homogeneous group of female returnees. In Hambantota husbands, fathers, mothers and sisters of migrants were interviewed when the migrant herself was still abroad. The majority of the respondents were in fact of this kind. The share of the nonmigrating households was also greater.

Consequently only a part of the sample (27 respondents) in Hambantota could be interviewed with the same systematic questionnaire used in Colombo. The rest of the sample (33 respondents) was interviewed in a more semisystematic way without the fixed questionnaire; therefore, these 33 households have not been included in the total sample of 139 that is processed statistically. This exclusion is a weakness in the sense that Hambantota's share of the total sample presented in the tables is fairly small (27 of 139). On the other hand, the semisystematic, more open interviews with relatives of the migrants provided new angles on the problem, adding dimensions and giving a fuller picture reflected in the general analysis. By and large, these interviews also confirmed, with some qualification, the impression arrived at through the interviews with the migrants themselves.

As mentioned, dropping in for only a few weeks to undertake interviews in an area certainly imposes serious limitations on the data that one obtains. Some of these limitations can be compensated for by preparatory study of background material specific to the area. As noted, available material from Hambantota is comprehensive and fairly rich. What proved equally important was background data achieved through informants of various kinds. Extensive use was made of local people familiar with the area, as well as historical and current knowledge about socioeconomic structures and behavioral patterns. Several persons had also taken a specific interest in the phenomenon of migration. Undoubtedly the most important source in this respect was the Planning Unit staff. Among others, the school supervisor, a local politician, some lawyers and members of the Grama Sevaka were interviewed.

Structure of the Book

A theoretical introduction to (1) the field of labour migration, (2) "gendered labour" and female migration in the Third World, and (3) labour migration in terms of human action is provided in Chapter 1. Two major approaches to labour migration in general are presented and discussed in terms of their relevance for the project. The distinctiveness of female migration is subsequently addressed in terms of gender theory on labour and subordination. Last, a synthesized approach is formulated, with emphasis on conditions for human action. The major hypotheses of the study are then presented in the context of the theoretical discussion.

The international and national settings for the project—the historical generation of labour migration from Sri Lanka to the Gulf—are presented in Chapters 2, 3, and 4. The supply (push) and demand (pull) sides of the migration link are dealt with in terms of the "international division of labour," with economic expansion and subcontraction of labour on the one end and recession and crisis in reproduction on the other. The more general statistical picture of the female migration is given to introduce the field.

In Chapter 5 the status of women in the sender society is examined: the traditional role of women in Sri Lanka according to class, ethnicity and religion. The changes over time in relation to women and work are examined in order to place labour migration in a historical context. The more striking aspects of female migration become apparent in light of the generally protected status of most Sri Lankan women.

Chapter 6 deals with the work status and the sociocultural status of the Sri Lankan women in the Gulf. It sketches the microsetting that confronts the individual migrant at her destination: What are her working conditions, her social environment and her rights while abroad?

In Chapter 7 the empirical findings from the two communities under investigation are presented and discussed.

In Chapter 8 the major discussion of consequences of female labour migration from Sri Lanka is presented. Special emphasis is placed on the cumulative results of the migration process in terms of macroeconomy, class and gender. Some concluding remarks are given with reference to the theoretical questions raised initially.

Notes

1. The words "Gulf" and "Middle East" will be used synonymously in this study. Both terms refer to the oil-exporting Arab countries in the Gulf region: Bahrain, Kuwait, Oman, Qatar, Saudi Arabia and the United Arab Emirates (UAE).
2. Throughout this study; US$1 = Rs 44.

1

Theoretical Approach to Labour Migration and Gendered Labour

Throughout history the movements of human populations have formed an inherent part of major processes of structural change. Such movements have taken numerous forms—as a response to political or economic pressure, spontaneous or coerced, involving large units like nations or smaller selected groups like minorities of various kinds. The movements have been temporary or more permanent, crossing local or national boundaries.

Since the advent of capitalism, particularly since the middle of the nineteenth century, one particular form of migration has become prevalent. This migration has the following main characteristics (Portes and Walton, 1981; Standing, 1985; Chapman and Prothero, 1983): First, it does not involve whole nations but only subsections of them. Second, it is not usually brought about through coercion but is induced structurally. The structural forces impelling migration are fundamentally economic; they reflect population pressure on resources, growing inability to meet local demands (often from exploiting elements) or generally a growing inability to reproduce the productive forces. Third and most important, this is migration of *labour* (that is, the movement is of individuals who are trying to sell their labour power in areas other than their home communities).

The word "migration" has become almost synonymous with this last kind of population movement—displacement of labour. And here the most extensively studied types are rural-urban and international migration. Although there has been an increase in literature on migration from low-income countries, the field still appears poorly covered in terms of theory and has been criticized for not having produced cumulative results: There is a prevalence of ad hoc explanations, a reliance on reductionist perspectives that preclude the analysis of macro-structural change and weakness as to political relevance and the ability to relate results derived from survey research to the general socioeconomic conditions in developing countries (Wood, 1982:299; Penninx, 1986).

The purpose of this chapter is to provide a general theoretical background for the determinants of labour migration and its implications for the people involved in order to place this case study within a broader, historical frame of reference. First, the two most prominent approaches to labour migration are presented: the microeconomic and the historical-structuralist approaches. The relevance of these two schools is discussed in relation to modern labour migration. I contend that the two approaches, having been de facto gender neutral, do not provide sufficient theoretical tools when it comes to understanding a gender-specific labour force. This criticism applies both to the causal and consequential aspects of the phenomenon. Theories of "gendered labour" and "subordination of women" in a Third World context are therefore presented as a third approach to the field.

All three theory complexes, however, have limitations as to the dimension of human action and decision-making. To give a more complete picture, I present a framework for understanding motivations, intentions, facilitators, barriers and individual strategies in concluding the chapter.

Two Major Approaches in Modern Migration Theory

Theoretical explanations of labour migration (which initially meant mostly rural-urban migration) date back at least to the 1880s, when E. G. Ravenstein (1885) presented his "law of migration." Ravenstein's theory has formed an important basis for migration research, and it has been evolved and systematized by many investigators. (See particularly Lewis, 1954; Lee, 1966.) The importance of economic motives in the decision to migrate, the negative influence of distance and the role of stepwise migration suggested by Ravenstein—all seem to be features that have not been invalidated by empirical research of more recent date.

Of the later theoretical work on labour migration, two major approaches or perspectives can be singled out, both of which include a fairly wide variety of subgroups. The first category is termed the *equilibrium model of migration* and the second, the *historical-structural perspective* (Wood, 1982). Later in this section I discuss the relevance of the approaches in relation to this study.

The Equilibrium Model of Migration

In this brief outline only an ideal type of the model is presented. Thus there is the risk of giving a rather crude and unnuanced version of this school of thinking. It is, however, beyond the scope of this work to elaborate further on the different tendencies and directions of the school. For further reading see Goldstein (1976) and Harris and Todaro (1970).

Some scholars claim that within the equilibrium perspective there is actually no need for a separate theory on migration, as migration is explained by the economic law of supply and demand (Nikolinakos, 1976). Even if neoclassical economists agreed with this basic assumption, considerable efforts have been made within this school to evolve analytical instruments in the field of migration. Sophisticated models have been generated to cover as many aspects of migration as possible at an aggregated level. The basic unit of analysis is, however, the individual. Migration flows are seen as the cumulative result of individual decisions based on rational calculations concerning costs and benefits.

In accordance with Ravenstein neoclassical economists claim that by redistributing human capital from places with low productivity to places of high productivity, migration contributes to development, correcting rural-urban, interurban and interregional imbalances in an economy. Temporary migration of labour power across national boundaries is also assumed to have the same effect. The geographical mobility of labourers is in itself a response to imbalances in distribution of land, labour, capital and natural resources, imbalances that influence the direction of the migratory flow. Labour moves from areas where capital is scarce and labour is abundant (and hence wages are low) to areas where capital is plentiful and labour is scarce (hence wages are high) (Wood, 1982).

Thus labour migration, according to this interpretation, serves as a mechanism that removes the existing disequilibrium between supply and demand in the international or national labour market. Labour migration is seen as having a stabilizing function in both the sending and the receiving society. Thus the flexible flow of workers serves as a buffer against social unrest in both ends. In the case of temporary labour migration the repatriates are also believed to serve as agents of change by contributing their newly acquired skills and ideas to the national development process. According to this model international labour migration therefore leads to a gradual convergence in the level of economic growth and social well-being (Wood, 1982).

The equilibrium model has been extensively criticized. By providing a highly formal theory of individual behaviour, the equilibrium model focuses on a common set of variables and generates hypotheses that can be tested through empirical research. Its critics assert, however, that the internal consistency of the model of individual decisionmaking is achieved at the expense of a broader understanding of the structural factors involved, concerning both the causes and the consequences of labour migration. It does not take into account the social relationships within the framework in which economic phenomena occur. People's basically rational behaviour is usually not questioned, in the sense that people's search for improvements in their lives can be a basic motivation behind geographical mobility. The neoclassical economists are rather accused of giving partial and ahistorical explanations, since they do not emphasize the role of noneconomic factors in the mobility decision and since they propose universal models that do not take into account the concrete structural changes that have taken place over the years relevant to labour migration.

The limitations of the equilibrium model are particularly evident with respect to the situation in developing countries. The macroeconomic stability supposed to result from the summation of individual self-interest has been seriously challenged from various development researchers (see, for example, Myrdal, 1957; Amin, 1974). Income differentials are not a cause in themselves but rather a symptom of structural inequalities between urban and rural (central and peripheral) areas, based on unequal allocation of resources (huge disparities in prices), exploitative land ownership systems and inappropriate technology. The disparities that led to migration in the first place have been accentuated rather than reduced, empirically speaking (Amin, 1974). What Gunnar Myrdal termed "cumulative causation" (Myrdal, 1957) applies directly to this phenomenon: Contrary to the assumption of a balanced economic development as a result of migration, research findings reflect a widening of the gap between senders and receivers. The inequality and the dependency is intensified through labour migration, according to these critics.

The Historical-Structural Perspective

This second theoretical approach has been developed largely as a critical response to the equilibrium model of migration. The approach is even more difficult to summarize in a fair way, as it comprises a wide variety of theoretical tendencies and milieus (see Wood, 1982). A common denominator is nevertheless that the perspective by and large is embedded in the Third World, the sender end of the migration flow, and that Marx's historical materialism forms the major theoretical basis from the outset.

Where the equilibrium tradition focuses on the rational calculation of the individual and treats migration as a discrete dimension of the general law of supply and demand, structuralists insist that population movements can be meaningfully analyzed only in the context of a historical structural transformation in a broad sense. Consequently the phenomenon of migration cannot be grasped without reference to a general theory of socioeconomic and political transformation of which it is a part.

Within the historical-structural approach two major tendencies stand out: the *dependency/world system model* and the *theory of articulation of modes of production.* Comprehensive works could easily have been written on both, judging from the vast quantity of material that has been produced within these approaches and the intense discussions that have been going on for years within and between the milieus. The presentation that follows is merely a crude version of the whole complexity.

Dependency/World System Approach. Central to the analysis from this perspective is the logical connection between the advent of capitalism and labour migration. Population movements have always accompanied major processes of structural change throughout history. The development of capitalism since the mid-nineteenth century, however, has given rise to a distinct, dominant mode of migration—labour migration. A major preoccupation for scholars belonging to this group is to show how migration is organically interconnected with the capitalist world system (see Bonacich and Cheng, 1984; Portes and Walton, 1981). It is taken as given that classes are defined by the social relations of production. Class structure is, in turn, conceptualized as an exploitative relationship that assures the unequal appropriation of natural resources and the value produced by human labour. The driving principle is capital accumulation and expansion on a world scale.

In contrast to microeconomic scholars structuralists explain population movements through pressures and counterpressures, both internal and external, on national economies that lead to transformation in the organization of production. The act of migration is not simply reducible to an individual's calculation of the costs and the benefits attached to the move; the individual's motivation is not sufficient to complete the act of migration. A distinction is drawn between individual motives for moving, regarded as secondary, and the structural changes that impel aggregate population movements. Accordingly labour migration is conceptualized as a class phenomenon, where the unit of analysis is the stream, rather than the sum of individual choices (Wood, 1982).

Unequal development is a key phrase in the historical-structural approach. The perspective suggests that the tendency for labour to move across boundaries correlates with a country's status in the world economy, whether it is located in the centre or the periphery of the global capitalist system. The centre (or core) is characterized by highly developed industrialized nation-states with diverse economic production and the periphery by weak nation-states specializing in the export of primary products. One of the most prominent scholars within the world system group, Immanuel Wallerstein, also operates with an in-between category—the semiperiphery—that has characteristics from both the core and the periphery (Wallerstein, 1974). The surplus labour and prevailing unemployment in sender countries are the results of low accumulation of capital and thereby economic backwardness coupled with a history of colonialism and dependence. These countries are not necessarily originally "poor in material riches and rich in human resources." They have become so because of dependency relationships enforced by powerful economic interests (Nikolinakos, 1976).

A main feature of the unequal exchange between the core and the periphery is global stratification of wage, with the consequence that workers in the centre receive much higher wages than in the periphery. The tendency to move from low-wage zones to the core is inherent; migration can be halted or encouraged depending on the conditions of the world market. The willingness of centre countries to accept population movements, according to these scholars, is the most crucial factor in determining prospects for international migration (Akinci, 1982). When the economic situation in the centre is expanding, migrants are likely to be in demand. During periods of recession, however, admission policies become more restrictive. The contradictory development of the capitalist system leads to these cycles of expansion and recession, with migrant labour providing a flexible stock of labour power and functioning as a "reserve army," according to structuralists.

The Articulation of Modes of Production. This tendency is a special branch of the Marxist-inspired historical-structuralist approach. The theoretical fundament of the branch is Marx's law of labour value and the concept of primitive accumulation. According to Marx the value of a commodity is determined by the labour time necessary for the production and, consequently, also the reproduction of a given article (Marx, 1867). Under capitalism labour power also becomes a commodity that can be bought and sold on the market. The value of the labour power is, according to Marx, the value of the means of subsistence necessary to maintain the labourer and his family. This value is determined concretely in a historical context through the power relations between the classes. An important distinction is made between the cost of reproduction of the labourer while he is in work and the cost of reproduction of the labour class as a whole. The first includes only the cost involved in keeping the labourer going while he or she is working, whereas the last means expenses also involving those parts of the labour class that are not productive: children, old people, the sick and unemployed.

These costs—the cost of total reproduction—are seen as necessary expenses for the capital in "pure" capitalist areas of production, where the labour power is completely "freed" from the means of production. This, however, is not the case where noncapitalist subsistence production exists beside the capitalist economy. In such cases the noncapitalist sector can provide labour power for the capitalists at the same time as it partly takes responsibility for reproducing the workers. This situation makes it possible for capital to pay labour power below its "formal value," according to the Marxist interpretation. The price of labour power is set lower than would have been necessary if capital had had to pay the whole cost of reproduction, meaning, in turn, that capital extracts a rent from the subsistence sector. A transfer of value from the noncapitalist sector to the capitalist sector consequently takes place. In other words, the noncapitalist sector subsidizes wages in the capitalist sector (Meillassoux, 1975).

The inherent precondition for this mechanism to take place is that the subsistence sector is preserved. It should not be fully integrated into the capitalist sector, yet it will have to be squeezed hard enough to create the need to take wage employment in the capitalist sector. It is this dynamic freeze of the relations of production that characterizes the "articulation of modes of production":[1] Dependence or a symbiosis is established between the two (or more) modes of production, although this relationship is asymmetrical. It is the capitalist mode of production that dominates once it is established and that profits from the relationship. Rotating or cyclical labour migration is probably the most characteristic manifestation of the articulation in concrete societies, with workers moving back and forth between the economically advanced sector and the semi–self-sustaining home areas. The migration in itself is seen as a symptom of such articulation.

This theory complex is most widely related to the situation in Africa and has played a significant role in developing an understanding of the structural causes and mechanisms operating in many societies on this continent.[2] Generally speaking, the theory is closely related to the discussion about development and underdevelopment.

Although the modes-of-production group of scholars comprises different tendencies and is marked by internal contradictions, we may view the articulation school as a response to, and possibly a synthesis of, two other branches of the world system approach: (1) The development optimistic tendency, with a basis in classical Marxism claims that capitalism functions equally everywhere in the sense that it breaks down noncapitalist modes of production and promotes development.[3] (2) The Dependencia group (or neomarxists) asserts that capitalism operates differently in the centre and the periphery, in the sense that the forces that promote accumulation and expansion in the centre function destructively and hamper potentials for development in the periphery (see, among others, Gunder Frank, 1971).

Common to both these tendencies is the presupposition that the driving forces in the world system come from the centre. The periphery is regarded as more or less as passive "recipients." Local structures and class relations are considered secondary and are given little attention.

Discussion. In contrast to these two perspectives, the mode of production theory at least opens up for studies of the developing countries themselves in a new way. A basic assumption is that traditional societies have a strong social and economic dynamic of their own, which influences the concrete form of society that is created through the interrelations between the modes of production. Hence the causes of underdevelopment lie not only in imperialism but to a certain degree also in the traditional societies themselves. The resistance in these societies against the process of dissolving themselves as self-reproducing units influences social formation for a lengthy transitional period, according to scholars of the articulation approach.

The various traditions within the historical-structural perspective have also been heavily criticized among themselves and from outside. Both broad groups presented here can be accused of being extremely abstract and consequently difficult to apply in any concrete socioeconomic context. Within this perspective very little field research has been undertaken to support the theoretical presumptions offered. T.J.F.A. Gerold-Scheepers and W.M.J. van Binsberger (1978) complain of the failure of Marxist scholars to "translate eloquent and illuminating abstractions into ordinary, prosaic case studies."

The microeconomic tradition has been particularly criticized for being reductionistic in its approach, that is, for not taking contextual factors into consideration. Structuralists fall into the opposite trap: Having identified the macrostructural forces that determine spatial imbalances in wages, employment and amenities, the historical-structural perspective pays very little attention to the factors that motivate individual actors. The individual migration tends to be conceptualized as an act to satisfy the abstract requirements of general laws of capitalist accumulation. These scholars implicitly take for granted that the decision to migrate is a rational one, but they make no contribution to our understanding of the decisionmaking process of individuals and households. Consequently they fail to explain which forces may influence the propensity to migrate and the direction of migratory streams. Because historical-structural literature has been developed in opposition to the individualism of neoclassical economics, it has tended to "search for the large-scale, long-term transformation of the global political-economy that, by definition, disregards the individual and the event" (Bach and Schraml, 1982:325). Nevertheless, this approach has served an important purpose by linking labour migration to concepts like imperialism, reserve army, international division of labour and world labour market.

Criticism of the mode of production perspective has followed somewhat different lines. Perhaps the most basic objection has come from Marxist sources, where it is argued that the theory is fundamentally of a functionalist kind, regarding economic and social mechanisms as well as individual behaviour only in terms of needs inherently contained in the capitalist mode of production. Concrete behaviour or transformations tend invariably to be traced back to these unquestioned "needs" of the system (functions without actors). This principle, in turn, gives the theory a touch of conspiracy according to some critics (Foster-Carter, 1978).

Another related major criticism concerns the possibilities of transcending the state of articulation into a "pure" capitalist society. The logic of the articulation of the modes of production implies a fairly stable situation—almost another kind of equilibrium—where the different modes of production play a complementary role, although to the benefit of the capitalist side, and the contradictions in the system tend to disappear. Some Marxists claim that the dialectics between conservation and dissolution of the noncapitalist mode of production that directs society into a qualitatively different stage conflict with the intrinsic functionalism of the approach (see Foster-Carter, 1978; van Binsberger and Meilink, 1978).

This presentation of the two major approaches and the critique against both has highlighted some basic differences with regard to (1) the object of inquiry (individuals versus structures) and (2) methodology (the model-building microeconomic method versus historical materialism; the study of the changing relations of production and class action on a global scale).

The differences also appear comprehensive with relation to the implications for theory of development and social change and for formulations of policies. The equilibrium tendency is often associated with the "modernization paradigm," having a positive evolutionist view on the direction of socioeconomic change. The role of migration in this context has been described as instrumental in a positive sense, through its assumed levelling function between sectors of different socioeconomic status, nationally or internationally.

The historical-structural block, on the other hand, tends to view migration in a negative perspective as a mechanism for exploiting countries and classes resulting from uneven development and the international division of labour. Even though individuals may profit from migrating in the short run, the consequences for the oppressed classes are unquestionably negative and serve to split the labouring masses on a global scale. The structural view of evolution is more blurred. Marxists are often described as "evolutionists" in the way they conceptualize the development of the productive forces through stages towards the ultimate communist society. This notion, however, is definitely "evolutionism" of a qualitatively different order than the one associated with the equilibrium perspective, since the two schools are based on entirely different analyses of the world economy, social structures and dynamics of change.

Gendered Labour Migration

So far we have dealt with labour migration in gender-neutral terms. We have looked at determinants and consequences basically in terms of economic and political macroforces. Since men and women hold quite different social and economic roles in society, an adjacent hypothesis would be that it is possible, at least in part, to distinguish gender-specific causes and consequences of labour migration. Do existing theories on the creation of a gender-specific labour force, class questions and the subordination of women within the household unit help to explain why and how women constitute an increasing contingent in labour migration? Do these theories represent alternative or complementary analytical tools to the traditional approaches?

It is necessary to discuss the connections between the internationalization of capital and the employment of a gender-specific labour force—why the work of lower-class women seems to be concentrated in certain economic sectors that are systematically weakly remunerated. The interaction of norms related to gender roles and the form women's labour takes in practice are relevant here: the close relationship between women's domestic role within the household, the specific kinds of work that are open for women in the labour market and the low value placed on female labour power in general.

Women as Subsidiary Workers

A substantial amount of work has been done on the question of the value of female labour power and the conditions determining the form of women's work. Main factors within the capitalist relations of production that make women's work "unpaid and invisibilised or poorly paid and marginalised" (Moser and Young, 1981) have been discussed under the label "women as subsidiary or secondary workers." Central questions are why the structure of qualifications in society is differentiated according to gender and why the forces of supply and demand systematically work to the detriment of women.

In developing, or less industrialised, societies the persistence of "pre-capitalist" subsistence production based on the household has been central to the question of capitalist development and the nature of transformation of the relations of production. Despite steadily more widespread capitalist penetration and commoditization, household subsistence economy and petty commodity production have shown resilience in both rural and urban societies throughout the Third World. The controversy referred to earlier over the conservation/dissolution dichotomy of these "pre-capitalist" forms of production has implicitly placed the domestic economy in a focal position within theories of underdevelopment.

Central to the discussion about sexual division of labour and women's subordination is the distinction between the sphere of production versus that of reproduction. Women's systematic assignment to positions with low pay, low skill and low status in society seems related to the fact that women are strongly identified with the *reproductive* side of this dichotomy. There appears to be a high congruence between the ideology of women as "naturally geared towards motherhood, wifehood and servicing others; naturally belonging to the realm of the home, the family, the minimal kin group, and their placement in the labour force" (Moser and Young, 1981). The concept of women as subsidiary workers—placed on a sidetrack of economic life and designated to certain sectors of the economy—would seem to stem from this ideology. The other side of this coin is the assigned "duty" of men to provide the means whereby women can undertake their reproductive obligations.

The ideological aspect of women's relation to the labour market has been emphasized in some recent theoretical works on women and development (see, for example, Rogers, 1980; Mies, 1986). Maria Mies's hypothesis is that women's work is never "free" in the Marxist sense, because even when women participate in wage labour, they remain bound up with extraeconomic relations of dependence or coercion. Mies points out that the Western influence in the Third World, apart from the direct economic impact, has been strong also when it comes to organization of the private sphere. The core-family model with a housewife and a male breadwinner has been transferred in the form of ideology to developing countries. The indirect effect has been to lower the remuneration for work undertaken by women in these areas also.[4]

Even though men may not be paid a wage that is in itself sufficient to support a family, the fact that their wages are still higher and the definition of women as dependents prevent women from gaining similar wages (Afshar, 1985). Women are paid less for comparable tasks, concentrated systematically in low-pay activities or hired on a different contractual basis, which implies a depression of wages compared to male earnings. Moreover, a large proportion of their daily undertakings are unpaid—both for the work that is carried out strictly for the maintenance and reproduction of the household and for work actually transmitted to the market. Unpaid family labour contributes significantly to the latter, either as part of peasant production or as an element of a wage-labour relation in which it is the male who is formally contracted (Redclift, 1985).

This condition underscores the general difficulty of distinguishing between women's productive and reproductive work. Domestic work tends to be an integrated whole, including physical reproduction and other aspects of the reproduction of the work force, as well as the production of use values and values for the market. Female work force participation thus has a tendency to concentrate in occupations delimited by ideology of gender, conditioned by the extent to which they are compatible with household obligations. Women's low pay derives, according to Kate Young (1978), not from economic dependence, as women are vital both to the reproduction and maintenance of labour, but from their "specialisation in reproduction" or the expectations surrounding it. "Their labour can thus be devalued both because of their 'real' role, and because this role itself places constraints on the type of work they can undertake." Women's bargaining power is consequently structurally reduced.

Women do participate also in the paid work force, although usually in work categories that are "part-time, often casual, unskilled, containing a truncated career structure, with weak or non-existing bargaining mechanisms; and in sectors which give little access to economic or political power" (Moser and Young, 1981). Women are also horizontally segregated into specific work categories that can often be seen as an extension of domestic labour into the market. This occurrence is partly contingent on the current life-cycle stage of the female worker. Young women without children may, for example, more easily take up work that is physically cut off from the household, like assembly line work for companies often placed far away from their communities.

Women's wage work is usually more discontinuous than men's, in the sense that it changes significantly over the life span. Rather than picturing women in developing countries as moving in and out of the labour market, it may be more fruitful to recognize that women most likely always work but along a scale with total wage employment at one end and unwaged, more reproductive work at the other. At different stages of their life cycle they move along this scale—the extent to which their work is remunerated will vary according to the stage. Both age and conjugal status are central determinants affecting the manner in which women work, the kinds of activities they are involved in and when this occurs (Moser, 1981:28).

The Household Unit in Studies of Female Migration

The household unit constitutes the closest context in which decisionmaking takes place in relation to labour migration.[5] The closest kin represents the structural and functional setting within which motivations and values are formed, information is received and interpreted and decisions put into operation.

For some researchers household studies have assumed a central status in "cross level analyses"—almost as a missing link between studies related to individuals and macrolevel approaches. The household unit is appraised as a context for understanding both structural and individual aspects of society—almost as a mediating entity that makes social action comprehensible through broader tendencies and processes of change in society at large. Relevant dimensions like economy, politics or international division of labour are related to a context that gives meaning to individual action.

The power relations within a household make this unit somewhat ambiguous when it comes to studies of gender questions and women's status in view of changing economic conditions. (See, for example, Young et al., 1981; Redclift and Mingione, 1985.) On the one hand, the socially constructed relationship between the sexes is seen as localized primarily in households, even though the functions and effects of gender relations cannot be explained without reference to society in totality. Control of women's labour and through that, control of reproduction (biologically and socially) becomes an essential element of the asymmetrical gender relations both within the household and concerning the role and function of the household in society at large. The household unit is thus viewed as the central arena where external and internal processes of female subordination are spelled out. The household, then, may provide a suitable unit of observation concerning gender-related issues.

On the other hand, the "household approach" in gender studies may have its pitfalls. Focusing on the household as the central unit of investigation can, ironically, sometimes lead to a gender-neutral approach. The woman is so closely identified with the household that the internal hierarchy along the sex and age dimensions disappears. This tendency has been prevalent particularly in many development aid programmes. In practice the household is regarded as a harmonious, collective unit with equal distribution of consumption, production and reproduction. This approach ignores the sometimes conflicting interests of its individual members, and the implicit assumption becomes that what is good for the household is good for all its members, including the women at different stages of their life cycle.

This implicit model in the realm of "women in development" has evoked considerable criticism, to the extent that the validity of using the household as an analytical unit as such has been questioned (see, for example, Harris, 1981). Obviously "the household" is no unitary social actor or decisionmaker anywhere. The household is a variable structure, both as a social unit cross-culturally and internally as a channel of broader social processes where separable, often competing interests, rights and responsibilities are spelled out.

Nevertheless, the household unit may still constitute a meaningful entity for studies of certain problems and relations in some concrete historical contexts. Households do exist in specific setups (which one has to uncover concretely) and provide a basis for the "social construction of reality" (Berger and Luckmann, 1979)—the forming of women and men as social persons. However, the ideology of the "family" in the Western sense also plays a role in its own right in many societies, either as a remnant from the colonial period or as a still-existing influence from the West. Thus this concept of the "family" functions somewhat as a "model" to these societies, even though this "ideal type" may be far from reality. Consequently this "interference" also has to be treated as a variable.

The assumptions made of the household as a "collective" decisionmaking unit, yet with unequal internal distribution of power, may have different implications as regards migration. This difference may concern the logic that motivates migration and the consequences for the woman herself. Presuming that it is increased (or maintained) well-being of the household that motivates the woman to move (not her individual striving), owing to the unequal distribution of power within the unit the outcome of her move may be different from that intended. For example, the male head of household may in practice use the money for other purposes. As to the consequences for the migrant herself, her own perception of the decisionmaking process may make a difference. If she sees the process as being "collective" or democratic, she may not feel overruled, even when the disposition of the money is to her objective disadvantage. In this case the migrant most likely will not oppose the basic sex role pattern already established in the migration process. If there is open disagreement (explicit conflicting interests) within the household, there will probably be stronger potential for change in terms of gender inequalities, or the oppression may be more explicit.

However, the household unit is in itself a rather unstable entity. It is subject to changes in its composition and function, due to general social processes, not least due to labour migration itself. These changes are themselves interesting subjects for inquiry. The complexity of the household's internal structure is an important aspect in the context of labour migration. The cash income that enters the household through this activity and the way in which it is controlled and distributed internally can shed light on the mechanisms that impose, reproduce or modify gender hierarchies. Changes in the sex role configuration as a possible consequence of this specific kind of separation can also be found in the household. Paradoxically a woman's absence as a migrant becomes a condition for her family's reproduction. At the same time this very absence may contribute to undermining the conjugal stability on which the household by definition is based.

A household approach in the context of particularly female labour migration must also open up for structural and concrete intrahousehold conflicts between women at different stages of the life cycle: mother/daughter, migrant/mother-in-law, migrant/migrant's mother.

Control over both women's labour and the biological reproduction of the family have been regarded as central concerns for the male heads of household (as well as for society at large) in many contexts. Traditionally the mobility of women has had to be restricted in order to sustain this control. Female migration therefore represents a drastic modification of this major concern. Control over women's labour in terms of day-to-day authority is obviously impossible. The woman is out of reach in a physical sense, which also means that direct control over her sexuality and hence reproduction is impossible. However, it should be stressed that "control" is a rather equivocal matter and can also be exerted without physical proximity. Psychological control may well be transferred to distant work sites. Command over remuneration can also be maintained through such mechanisms. Concerning biological reproduction of the family, female migration can represent a threat, depending on where in the life cycle the migrant woman is and how lasting the separation is. The potential demographical effect of female migration is a major concern to national authorities where such migration occurs.

Female international labour migration represents a major break with tradition in many respects in the societies concerned and embodies potentials for change in male-female relations. However, there is also the possibility that traditional sex roles and perceptions do not change but instead become reintegrated in a new fashion into the altered situation. The new situation will, in any case, generate new configurations of strains and conflicts that should be investigated.

Continued Subordination or Emancipation?

The increased use of female labour power in wage employment in the wake of the restructured international economy has naturally engendered discussion as to the potential for "liberation" of women.[6] Increased female participation in the labour market could imply stronger economic independence and a life outside the household and could thus be envisaged as having "liberating" potential. This discussion, which dates back to the industrial revolution of the last century in Europe, is difficult, both conceptually and empirically. Such "liberation," apart from the philosophical aspects of the matter, is extremely hard to measure or grasp concretely. Nevertheless, the attempt has been a central preoccupation as a perspective when the role of women in various societies has been analyzed.

In this context we have focused on a new kind of wage employment for women, in which the link between the internationalization of capital and a gender-specific labour force is specifically clear. As indicated, even though women's ascriptive roles may not be compatible with intensive wage employment on assembly lines, in the tourist sector or in domestic work in another country, the urgent need for cash can cause deeply rooted traditional ideas to be put aside or to be redefined.

It is the argument of this book that although forms of work are directed by economic structures and ideological systems, women should not be seen solely as passive agents of these forces, or victims of circumstances. Action eventually implies choice, however structurally directed. Thus even though women enter the labour force with a predefined status as "inferior bearers of labour" (Redclift and Mingione, 1985), employment may offer them certain advantages and may represent a basis for improving their total life situation. Employment outside the home at least gives women a partial distance from the confines and dictates of the traditional male-dominated social relations, and it may also give them some kind of status. Work is not merely an economic activity; It expresses a relationship between people and has important symbolic aspects as well.

The work relation for these Third World women consequently embodies an important ambiguity in terms of emancipation/subordination: On the one hand, the women are conferred a degree of economic independence that to a certain point may improve their status in the family. At least they are no longer "just another mouth to feed." They have more personal freedom of action, and they have access to new kinds of experience and activities. (Indeed, having a position in the wage labour force is generally viewed by the women themselves as "liberating" [Heyzer, 1986:110].) On the other hand, their actual work usually implies a high degree of exploitation. They remain at the bottom of the hierarchy, with the lowest pay, often with extremely poor working conditions and with little control over their own situation. Historically this is not unique; there seems to have been a tendency whereby "exploitation and liberation go hand in hand" (Lim, 1983) along with developing economic space for women.

Studies on female participation in the work force in the Third World tend to put less emphasis on the emancipatory side of this ambiguity "since there is nothing emancipating in bad conditions, low wages, overwork, humiliation and discrimination" (Morokvasic, 1984:129). Whatever extra space women may gain from their wage employment, it is often said to represent a "pseudo-emancipation," if any emancipation at all. It is said to create a false climate for liberation, not surpassing an increased purchasing power. The freedom gained is merely a freedom to consume more (Abadan-Unat, 1986).

Even though this conclusion may be empirically correct in some cases, it is important not to have this as a preconceived notion. To avoid the pitfall of structuralism, the possibility of improvement—also in the realm of women's status—should be kept open. The extent of women's liberation does not depend solely on restrictions created by macrolevel structures. A more complete picture emerges when we emphasize the influence of action upon these structures.

The question of role conflict is central to any substantial investigation of changing conditions for women in the wake of stronger participation in wage employment. Modernization is often identified with the creation of new role conflicts for women, as income-generating work represents a competition with maternal responsibilities. These conflicting pressures cannot be understood in terms of traditional perceptions of women. The way the economic demands on women are justified on the ideological level and the way traditional patterns of authority and control are "de-composed" or "re-composed" vary from society to society. Consequently these processes represent interesting scenarios for research.

Theories at Different Levels

Many scholars have realized the importance of contextual factors when studying motivation and behaviour in relation to labour migration. In particular, researchers working at the community/household level are highly aware of how poor are predictions of labour migration when considered predominantly from aggregated levels or from a purely economic angle. In this context Cardona and Simmons (1975) have pointed out that "many men have relatively poor job opportunities in rural areas, but only some individuals go to the city."

However, social and cultural factors have rarely occurred in the models that predominate in international migration studies. The common pattern in migration models is to use employment levels, job opportunities, wage rate differentials, cost of moving and availability of employment as explanatory variables. Any variance that remains unexplained by these models is then attributed to "contextual factors" that remain external to the models (Hugo, 1981).

Some of this "model weakness" is understandable, given the scarcity of research results concerning the social and cultural factors that influence migration decisions and not least the difficulties involved in identifying and specifying the precise nature of such influences (as opposed to influences from other factors). These sociocultural factors are generally also difficult to quantify, which makes them less attractive to include in model-based research.

I contend that none of the three approaches presented can be considered satisfactory as theoretical tools when it comes to establishing the determinants of labour migration in a broad sense. All these schools have their historical merits in providing thoroughly different perspectives on the issue and in uncovering mechanisms that tend to act similarly in different socioeconomic conditions: the equilibrium school with its emphasis on the rational choice of the individual; the historical structuralists with the economic macroforces and the structural context in focus. None of the approaches, however, provide sufficient means to understand the complex motivation structure at the individual level nor the interplay between the intentional actor and the institutional setting.

On the consequence side I also contend that the three schools have major limitations. Since none of the theories really handle motivation in relation to a sociocultural setting, the tools for understanding consequential behaviour and impact on individuals/households and communities are not provided either.

This concrete case study aims at explaining and analyzing female migration on different levels of abstraction and from different conceptual angles. Thus theoretical tools are needed from varied sources. At the international level we need concepts to handle aspects of the world economy that can explain the systematic movements of people looking for work. What international economic and social forces influence the propensity to migrate and the direction of the migration streams?

We need conceptual means to understand the socioeconomic changes that have impelled labour migration and the major barriers and pitfalls involved. Regional differences, level of modernization, land questions and job opportunities are relevant variables in this respect. These factors call for explanations derived from the political economy of production and distribution. In this macroterrain the historical-structural approach has important contributions, as we have seen so far.

We also need a conceptual framework (1) for human action and (2) for action in terms of gender (socioeconomic preconditions for a gender specific pattern of action). We need to identify people having motives and interests and to locate the contradictions that may exist between actors and groups of actors. We need to encounter the way in which time, space and society selectively influence the actor and are reflected in the actor and, simultaneously, how the individual actor feeds back into society and thereby reproduces and/or transforms it. This means discovering the actors beyond the functions they may serve by searching for, on the one hand, the conditions for human action and, on the other hand, the way in which the actors influence society by their aggregated behaviour. In this way, society continuously represents living historical aggregates, where yesterday's actions become today's context for conscious behaviour.

More than new theoretical paradigms, this complex calls for concrete analyses that try to link and combine the different approaches and levels of analysis.

Labour Migration in Terms of Determinants

Examining human action in relation to labour migration is actually a process through which we translate the structural setting into relevant considerations for individual decisionmaking: Which macrofactors do individuals consider important and as impinging upon their reality?

There is an important distinction between the determinants and the consequences of migration. Determinants concentrate on the initiators of action, whereas consequences relate to adjustments and responses to the behaviour.

Determinants

A basic assumption in this context is the rationality of the decisionmaker. The potential migrant is assumed to be acting rationally and intentionally upon a set of options or forces in the perceived surroundings. According to J. Elster (1979), an act is "rational" if it is the best means to realize the set goal. Rationality is relative, however, in the sense that it is based on the quality and quantity of information available, the individual's perception of this information and the specific preferences of the actor. Information may be accurate, incomplete or based on deliberate falsifications. Preferences, on the other hand, may predispose the actor towards a particular option. A basic precondition when speaking of "rational choice" is that there actually are realistic alternatives to choose between.

Motivation is a key word in this respect, as it comprises the constituting elements in the decisionmaking process: needs, values, perceptions, customary practices and aspirations. One way or another, motivation has to be present for an act to take place. As we have seen, the equilibrium school confined motivational structure solely to economic variables in terms of cost-benefit and supply-demand dichotomies. Although these variables are usually central in analyses of labour migration, they do not reflect the total context of the decision to move. They may also be quite inadequate for distinguishing movers from stayers (De Jong and Fawcett, 1981). Other motives behind labour migration might include social status attainment (in a broad sense), escape from social misery, family reunification, self-realization and life-style preferences. The motivation behind a move may be said to be based on a continuous evaluation of the total life situation at home (level of stress/satisfaction, cost-benefit calculations, values and expectations) in relation to opportunity structure (demand), eventually depending on information available to the potential migrant.

The action of migration could then be explained according to the following model: (1) The social background of the migrant provides perceptional filters that in turn explain the specific preferences of the actor (various intentions may lie behind the same act of migration); (2) the structural context (societal forces at large) explains the formation of possibilities; and (3) the preferences and the formation of possibilities together explain the intentional action (Elster, 1979). Additionally, action by a number of individuals may change the structural context as well as the norms and values that influence perception in society. Action is thus seen as governed by an interplay of motivational factors and structural conditions in a concrete context. In the decisionmaking process, constraints and facilitators will influence this interplay.

Let us briefly outline the major facilitators and constraints (and some ambiguous categories) that may influence decision-making in relation to international labour migration in a Third World context. Constraints can also help to explain nonaction in this respect. (The factors will presuppose that the demand is there.)

Facilitators. Access to information and, in turn, recruitment agencies are necessary preconditions. Migration networks in local communities may play an important role in this respect. Furthermore, improved transportation connections will increase possibilities (particularly overseas migration) and efficiency and favorable government policies towards export of labour may propel the process. Last, extended family support will alleviate burdens connected with the move.

Constraints (Subjective or Objective). First and foremost, the initial cost of obtaining a contract may limit the possibilities of going, as will family obligations at home. Distance to work site and consequently the time (and cost) factor relating to home visits can discourage migration. Remoteness of home area may imply constrained access to information and agents. Strangeness or alienness of foreign culture can also be perceived as a major barrier, and finally, the age factor may represent an impediment (the prospective candidate may be too old, according to rules).

Ambiguous Categories. Some other factors may work both ways depending on the concrete circumstances. Community norms may both facilitate and constrain migration and may change over time. These norms are usually gender specific. Big families may imply bad economy and compel migration, but family obligations may make a move difficult. This constraint should particularly be so for women. Bonds of affection to family may make it difficult to part, but the sacrifice of going is meaningful.

Effects on Behaviour

The second part of the theory complex relates to the indirect effects of the act of migration—the adjustments and responses.

In a similar vein as we saw on the causal side, the effects of labour migration will be determined by a combination of conscious decisionmaking and structural conditions that impose themselves on the actor. Consequences can be both intentional and unanticipated. Migration will always have fairly strong elements of risk-taking behaviour, considering all the noncontrollable factors. The risk may be calculated or unidentified. Unanticipated consequences may also be a result of misinterpreting objective conditions, in the sense that the preconditions for the decisionmaking did not prove to be there.

It may be useful to analyze consequences at different stages of the action process. This analysis may be particularly relevant in relation to labour migration that often is cyclic, in that the migrant leaves for work repetitively. Had the migrant left the first time in order to find her/his economic feet more permanently, then the aim would not have been accomplished if he/she would have to go again. Along the chain of actions, the results of the first decision may become structural, in that the preconditions for moving reproduce themselves. Alternatively, the results of the first move may cause different behaviour, owing to the element of learning in the process. The original causes may also have changed along the way. Migrant number 1 may leave an area for reasons quite different from those of number 36,000 some five years later—not least because the added actions of that many people will change the scene. Thus we may have a scale of consequences where learning and changed basic preconditions (including the action of migration itself) form important parts of the process.

The analysis of effects of migration therefore becomes relevant for the causal theory in two ways: first, to see whether the results of the migration correspond to the anticipated implications of the causal theory, and second, to decide whether the results contribute to the reproduction or reinforcement of the original causes or whether they generate new reasons along the way.

Conclusions and Analytical Problems

I have in this chapter presented and discussed two established approaches to labour migration—the equilibrium theory and the historical-structuralist theory. I concluded that although the schools can contribute in a very general sense, providing a conceptual framework, they also have major limitations.

First, the approaches are gender neutral, which—at least in our context—means that they do not contribute to an understanding of gender-specific aspects of labour migration. Second, the two main approaches lack a conceptual command over the field of human action and decisionmaking processes and the interplay between these factors and the institutional setting.

In the last two sections of this chapter I have consequently presented and discussed (1) central fields and aspects of gender that are relevant to the study of labour migration and (2) a conceptual framework for analyses of motivational factors in relation to institutional/structural conditions in society. I contend that a combination of different theoretical perspectives is necessary for our purposes.

On the basis of the theoretical assumptions discussed in this chapter, the following problems and theoretical questions direct the empirical part of the study (more operationalized problems will be presented later).

First, I will describe and analyze how changes in the international economy and the political economy of Sri Lanka have affected living conditions for common people and in turn laid the foundation for the exodus of the female migrants from the island.

Concerning the basic intentions of the migrating women, I hypothesize that the general desire is to improve or maintain the quality of life for the whole family. This basically economic motive may have different implications depending on the rationale upon which the migrants act and the preconditions in society:

- Is the search for employment abroad a response to a crisis in subsistence of the family, or does it aim explicitly at economic investment and mobility? In other words, does the move reflect a structural adaptation, or is it part of a conscious strategy or plan?
- Do the female migrants follow basically a bread-winning logic for the family as a collective, or do they also have their individual ambitions and desires? Do they conceive of the traffic to the Gulf as an opportunity or an obligation and a sacrifice?
- If there are female migrants from other social strata than the lower groups, are there significant differences in motivations and aspirations?

On the effect side, I will first analyze the intended and unintended consequences of labour migration for the Sri Lankan state in terms of foreign income generation, alleviation of unemployment and dissatisfaction among the citizens and possible long-term dependence.

As the clear majority of the female migrants are recruited from the poorest strata of the population, one would assume that (at least) two years with a considerable income compared to what they are used to could give them a significant social uplift. In other words, such female Middle East migration could function as a vehicle for social mobility:

- If this is so, does the group of women going to the Gulf function as an agent of change that may promote economic growth and enhancement of social well-being in the local communities? Or does such migration only generate further dependency on different levels in society?
- If social improvement is not accomplished, what are the unanticipated consequences, and why did they come about? Is the rationale upon which the migrants act undermined by the fact that the preconditions in society for a successful result do not prove to be there?
- Has any learning followed by changed behaviour taken place that affects future preconditions for moving? In other words, do the migrants contribute to the formation of a new social and economic environment that generates other options and motivation patterns, or do the results contribute to the reproduction and/or reinforcement of the original causes?
- To what degree are the possible unintended consequences gender and class specific?

Concerning the potential for reduced subordination, entering paid employment is a condition for access to more independence. Major clusters of old social, economic and psychological commitments can be eroded, since people are structurally directed into new patterns of socialization and behaviour. Although there is abundant evidence worldwide that there is no easy and direct relationship between independent employment and relief from subordination, the female Middle East migration involves such a drastic challenge of traditional norms and values that some change in this respect would be expected.

- If there are some changes in gender relations locally, what expressions do they take, and how lasting are they likely to be? If no changes are noted, why is that so?

Before relating these hypotheses and questions to the microdata from two Sri Lankan communities, I will give a background description of the context in which the migration takes place. First, relevant forces on the international and national scene will be presented and discussed (Chapters 2, 3 and 4). Then a discussion of women's status—in the traditional society and in the setting to which they migrate—is presented in Chapters 5 and 6.

Notes

1. It is beyond the scope of this work to elaborate any further on various Marxist concepts like relations and modes of production. Different scholars use the concepts differently, which also makes it difficult to single out one representative version.

2. Documentation within this theoretical branch is vast. Let the following suffice: Amin, 1976; Cliffe, 1978; Foster-Carter, 1978; Kerven, 1980; Meillassoux, 1975; Murray, 1981; Taylor, 1979; Wolpe, 1980.

3. Bill Warren is a commonly cited proponent of this view (Warren, 1973).

4. This field of "domestic labour" and the existence of a "family wage" has been the subject of much discussion within the Marxist tradition of gender studies. (See, among others, Edholm et al., 1977; Harris and Young, 1981; Molyneux, 1979; Beneria, 1982; and Young et al., 1981.) The attempt by Marxist feminists to theorise domestic labour and women's wage work in light of capitalist accumulation is part of the aim of relating sexual division of labour to the labour process at large. The core of the debate is the question whether a wage in capitalist societies is supposed to take care of the full reproduction of the whole family of the paid worker, which by definition is said to be the value of the labour power in Marxist terms. The analytical strength of the concept of "family wage" or, indeed, the real existence of the phenomenon is strongly questioned, particularly pertaining to conditions in developing countries. As B. Bradby asks, "how could one maintain a labour theory of value in face of the recognition that the labour of half the world did not take the form of value?" (Bradby, 1982).

5. *Household unit* as an analytical concept is of a rather loose character. It seems essentially based on a residential criterion, a unit in which the production and exchange of goods and services are primarily organized through relations of kinship, most often the conjugal pair. What is generally meant are those people who share a domestic economy, often actually a common cooking pot (Moser and Young, 1981). *Family* is often used synonymously. As this broad definition becomes somewhat ambiguous when it comes to certain kinds of migrant households, it can be useful to stress the economic side rather than the co-residential, as central members of the family often will be more or less permanently absent. Colin Murray sees it as a "functional manifestation in terms of income-generating activities" (Murray, 1981:48).

6. *Liberation* and *emancipation* are pretentious words, which in their full meaning probably are beyond reach, be it in the Third—or First—World. Such terms therefore have to be understood in a relative way. In this context they are used rather loosely in the sense of making life better, more independent and more dignified for the women in question.

2

The Receiving Side—The Gulf

The historical development of the Gulf region provides a central background to the understanding of labour migration from Sri Lanka (and Asia in general) to the respective countries in the area. The Gulf as a region represents the demand—or pull—side of the migration link and thus constitutes a necessary precondition for the traffic in the first place.

International labour migration is not a new phenomenon in the Gulf region. It has grown steadily since World War II. However, since the early 1970s there has been a profound change in the nature and scale of this migration. The cause of this shift was the oil-price explosion of 1973–74 and the vast increase in revenues that followed in the Gulf states: Kuwait, Bahrain, Qatar, the United Arab Emirates (UAE), Oman and Saudi Arabia.

This sudden prosperity triggered a rapid economic and social transformation that called for labour power in a wide range of activities. First, the process of further resource exploration, drilling of wells, construction of pipelines and terminals, as well as related facilities within the fields of infrastructure, required excess labour. Second, most of these countries wanted to develop quickly for their citizens a high level of welfare services, like schools, clinics and hospitals. Developments of this kind, being predominantly labour intensive, required large supplies of various kinds of labour power, hardly any of which was to be found within the states themselves.

In the early 1970s most Arab countries could be described as developing in an economic and social sense. Even the most capital-rich countries at that time were "underdeveloped" in terms of some central measures like literacy (Birks and Sinclair, 1980).[1]

The Labour Market in the Gulf

The Gulf countries were also invariably sparsely populated and had a very low rate of female employment. The low participation of women in the labour market is partly a result of social and religious customs that restrict females in working outside the home, except in a limited number of professions like teaching and nursing and within certain women's organizations (Birks and Sinclair, 1980:20).[2] Consequently the labour power demand that followed from the comprehensive new development projects of the different governments had to be met from abroad.

In the beginning of the new oil era this demand was mainly met from the poorer Arab countries, which traditionally had provided any extra labour power needed in the Gulf. Soon after the boom started, this contingent was, however, supplemented by a steadily increasing flow of male workers from Turkey, Iran, Afghanistan, South Korea, the Philippines, Thailand, Malaysia, Indonesia, India and Sri Lanka.

The new tendency of recruiting Asians instead of other Arabs was brought about partly because Asian labour was cheaper and partly because some of the former supplier countries (particularly Iran and Iraq) began to develop their own economies, which made remaining in the national labour markets more attractive to their workers than migrating to the oil-rich Gulf states (Birks and Sinclair, 1980:29). It could also have been a deliberate policy on the part of the oil-rich states to diversify the supply side, not to depend on any single source or even a few sources that could form a cartel (Nagi, 1986). Another important factor behind the change in the composition of foreign labour was that non-Arabs were considered less of a risk politically. The regimes of the oil-rich states had presumably calculated that their leverage over non-Arabs would be greater than over Arabs and therefore opted for gradually replacing the potentially politicized Arabs with more obedient and politically docile Asian workers (Nagi, 1986). Arabs, being familiar with the language, religion and also culture, had found ways of staying for lengthy periods of time, bringing their families with them and thereby also exerting a burden on the infrastructural facilities of the countries. When Asian workers entered the scene, Gulf labour policies had been restructured so that workers were allowed to stay for only a fixed period of time—the period of their work contract. The labour force was heavily controlled, mostly being confined to isolated areas near the work sites. Workers were not allowed to bring their families, a restriction that also reinforced the transient character of their stay. The reproductive responsibility of the recipient governments was consequently minimized.

By the early 1980s there were some 6 million foreign workers in the Gulf region, of whom approximately 2 million were Arabs and about 3.7 million were Asians.[3] The remainder came from Africa. (In 1970, in comparison, about 660,000 migrant workers were occupied in the region [Owen, 1986].[4]) Of the total labour force in the region, something like 70–80% came from abroad. In Kuwait, the UAE and Qatar migrant workers make up more than 50% of the total population (Halliday, 1984).

During the 1970s the expatriate labour force in the Gulf was predominantly composed of males—contract workers who served as a "temporary construction crew" (Zahlan, 1984). Along with the rapid economic transformation these societies underwent in this period, the life-style of ordinary people was also subject to change. The middle class grew significantly, and more people achieved a higher standard of living. With this more affluent style came a growing demand for servants, nannies and cooks in a broader spectrum of Arab households. As mentioned, the rate of female employment in the Gulf has been very low and still is one of the lowest in the world. Only a very few occupations are considered appropriate for women, paid housework definitely not being one. And so migrant labour also turned out to be a cheap, convenient response to this specific demand—in this case the migrant workers were predominantly Asian females.

Only in one of the Gulf countries has this import of labour been accompanied by a significant increased participation of the indigenous female work force, namely, in Bahrain (Franklin, 1985). In 1981 the country employed 7,200 personal servants, of which 97% were non-Bahraini. This figure has increased substantially since, and Asian (particularly Sri Lankan) housemaids have become commonplace also among groups that had never employed servants. Of the approximately 6 million foreign workers in the Gulf, 20% are estimated to be maids. This figure means that in the region there are several times more foreign servants alone than there are citizens in Qatar, for example.

Working Conditions in the Oil-rich Gulf States

Common to the vast majority of the foreign workers in the Gulf area is their lack of protection. They lack clearly defined rights; local courts and administrative procedures are ineffectual, and foreign workers are dependent on the goodwill of their institutional or individual sponsors. Most Asian migrants are subject to local labour laws that insist that all foreigners be imported on a short-term basis, generally through a fixed contract for no more than two years. Their task during the stay is clearly specified, and they can change employers only with the permission of the first sponsor. When the contract period is over, their work permits and visas automatically expire at the same time. Moreover, any foreigner can also be deported at any time by local ministers of the interior, all of whom seem to have been given carte blanche where national security is concerned. Only in Bahrain does there seem to be a right of appeal (Owen, 1986). The one Gulf state with legal trade unions is Kuwait, but foreigners are allowed to join only after five years' residence.

As to the wage conditions there is a three-tier system with European expatriates at the top, Arabs in the middle and Asians at the bottom. At present Bangladeshi and Sri Lankans tend to get the very lowest salaries. National wage levels in the respective sender countries influence the level at which labour is offered, but certain prejudices also seem to be a source of inequality. For instance, Iranian and Afghan unskilled labourers are believed to work harder than anyone else, and Filipino housemaids are assumed to be "cleaner" than others. Both these categories are paid higher salaries than equivalent groups from other countries (Owen, 1986).

Among the foreign workers in the Gulf possibly the most vulnerable category of all is that of the female domestic servants. For these women, isolated in the private households where they work, external protection is virtually nil. Even existing local labour laws specifically exclude domestic work from their sphere of influence. Registration of abuses and maltreatment of various kinds is consequently extremely difficult. Some of the cases have been registered, as women once in a while seek refuge in their country's embassy—if there is one. Another indication is provided by advertisements in Gulf newspapers asking for information concerning "run-away" servants. These more visible aspects of the problem probably show only the tip of an iceberg.[5]

Foreign Labour—Effects in the Gulf

Reliance on foreign labour in national economies to the extent evident in the Gulf area obviously has economic and social implications for the host countries.[6] On the one hand, they could not possibly have seen the growth rates and the development projects that have been realized without this foreign contribution. Foreign workers have helped them translate the huge oil revenues into higher standards of living for their citizens. On the other hand, they are increasingly becoming aware that this factor has created a dependency and consequently a vulnerability in the system.

The transience of the oil wealth is probably the most frightening element of the economic scenario for Gulf governments, as long as they do not manage to diversify their economies in depth. The dominant tendency so far has been to create enclave economies preoccupied with construction and service activities, with heavy state involvement. There has been a dangerous neglect of agriculture, and industrial development has mostly been restricted to a few capital-intensive enterprises (Halliday, 1984).

Easy access to foreign labour in the growth sectors has also created an employment pattern within the countries that may prove harmful when the foreign workers are, at least to a certain extent, to be replaced by local labour power. The host countries have clearly perceived the migrants as a necessary evil, temporarily present to undertake basic construction work in the takeoff stage of their economies. An indication of this is the systematic segregation of the migrants from political and social life in the host countries (Richards and Martin, 1983).[7] The oil boom has made the nationals a "labour aristocracy," mostly occupied with well-paid trade and public service activities, directly benefiting from the foreign presence. Over the years this situation has eroded the work motivation in the indigenous population, so that at present there are many jobs that locals are unwilling or unable to perform. Governmental efforts to train the local labour force in the skills needed to replace the foreigners have achieved little success so far. (Owen, 1986).

Although major changes have been taking place in the Gulf societies since the oil revenues started flowing, the new prosperity has also helped to preserve central social and cultural traits, like the custom of keeping women outside the labour market. Hence the concept of labour shortage is a relative one, as long as this huge potential is kept passive. As mentioned, Bahrain is to a certain extent an exception, as a significant number of Bahraini women have entered the labour force since the oil boom. The interesting factor in this context, is that this radical change has so far not been accompanied by serious conflicts in the private sphere. The main reason seems to be the availability of cheap household labour from abroad: "Increasing numbers of Bahraini women can work, or spend time visiting or entertaining, without affecting their traditional roles as housewives and mothers. Servants are available to cook, clean and take care of the children while the Bahraini women engage in other activities" (Franklin, 1985:10).

The importation of (mostly Sri Lankan) housemaids has consequently contributed both to a major change in the socioeconomic situation of Bahraini women and to the continuity of central values in society. Social relations, cultural orientations and the politics of the family have not been basically challenged. The availability of foreign maids has also so far prevented the "mechanization" of household labour seen in the West (Franklin, 1985).

At the same time foreign labour as such is clearly seen as a major cultural threat to society at large in the Gulf. Keeping the foreign workers as distant as possible from the daily lives of the Arab community is one way of trying to reduce this threat. With housemaids, however, this separation is not possible, owing to the nature of the job. Increasing concern has also been expressed from the Arab side as to the continuation of the Arab-Islamic upbringing of their children in the wake of the "housemaid-invasion" from other cultures. Therefore, preference for Muslim foreign women has been a significant feature on the demand side, representing an attempt at least to neutralize the religious factor.[8]

There are a number of uncertainties involved concerning the future of the labour market in the Gulf states, the most basic one being the source of the wealth itself—oil revenues. Both the magnitude of the resource base and, not least, international oil prices are critical factors in this respect. "Indigenization" has become the theme in all the host countries, even though only Saudi Arabia has followed up with sizable reductions in the number of foreign workers. The work-force question is loaded with conflicting aims, as the various governments are increasingly coming to realize. Social tensions are being created, as mentioned above. The question is whether the historical connection between expatriate labour and development can be discontinued or, at least, reduced. To bring about this outcome, there are at least three options: (1) The economies of the Gulf states may be transformed, so that the productive sector remains, but with the amount and quality of services provided for the citizens reduced drastically; (2) foreign workers may be granted citizenship; (3) the current situation can be maintained (Owen, 1986). None of these options appears to fulfil all requirements satisfactorily as far as the governments are concerned.

At the same time, it seems that the foreign presence will have to be reduced, owing to the economic decline; likewise, the standard of living of the indigenous population inevitably must be lowered in the future. World Bank economist Naiem Sherbiny (1984) has tried to calculate the future labour market needs of three Gulf states (Saudi Arabia, Kuwait and the UEA), based on a "medium growth scenario." The short-term implications for the work force will, according to these calculations, probably be a drop in construction employment. This reduction might be compensated for by expanding the labour needed for maintaining and operating the projects. Such a shift would however, require a different skill composition, with greater emphasis on trained labour.

Concerning the foreign housemaids, Sherbiny does not expect a rapid decline in recruitment. Rather, the opposite—he expects a short-term increase. If, however, the standard of living of the Arab population will have to decline, this specific demand will most likely be affected, although with some time lag.

A constituting feature of the labour migration to the Gulf is that it does not take place primarily between structurally less developed countries to more developed areas, as has been the case with migration to Europe and the United States, currently and historically. The Gulf states are rich in money but poor in development—so far. The migrants have moved to rent-collecting, not highly industrialized, economies (Richards and Martin, 1983), implying that the recipient countries may shut the door to outsiders once they have reached a certain level of development.

The discussion in this chapter has focused on the setting in the recipient end of the migration, revealing a complex picture of conflicting considerations. The picture at the other end is no less complex. What is called "the expatriate time bomb" in the Gulf (Nagi, 1986) also has its explosive side in the sender countries—in this case, Sri Lanka.

In Chapter 3 the basic features of this sender economy will be spelled out, as part of the general international setting, to describe the background to female labour migration from Sri Lanka on an aggregated level. There is in this context no ambition to cover the history of Sri Lanka but simply to indicate in what direction we might look for relationships between socioeconomic development and behaviour of individuals.

Notes

1. At the beginning of the 1980s Kuwait still had a literacy rate of 55% (Birks and Sinclair, 1980).

2. Women constitute an essential part of the work force, however, in the poorest sections of these societies, as elsewhere. Although the very strict Muslim norms as to a woman's behaviour and economic activity confine her to the home, small-scale agriculture in many of the countries (e.g., Oman, Yemen and parts of Saudi Arabia) depend upon female labour. (Jørgensen and Mønsted, 1983).

3. Asians workers are found mostly in the countries where economic development is most recent and least mature (Birks and Sinclair, 1980).

4. All figures in this section should be handled with caution, as statistical estimates are of variable quality.

5. The only way to get an impression of the real work situation for these women is to undertake interviews directly with the maids. Findings from such interviews are presented later in this book.

6. This could constitute a major research topic in itself. In this context, however, it is slightly off the main track. Only some aspects of the scene that are linked to the prospects for further migration from Asia and Sri Lanka will therefore be included in this section.

7. Fred Halliday also indicates at a more *political* aspect of the policy from the outset: In Oman, the promotion of migration was, according to political opponents of the regime, a means of avoiding the creation of an indigenous working class (Halliday, 1984:6).

8. This tendency has also implied changes in recruitment from Sri Lanka, with more and more housemaids coming from a Muslim background. This topic will be dealt with later in the book.

3

The Sender Side—Sri Lanka

The oil-price boom in the Gulf in the early 1970s was a basic precondition for the comprehensive labour migration traffic from various Asian countries to the oil-rich Gulf states. Without this active demand for labour power in large quantities, the migration bridge would not have been created. This demand is, however, not a sufficient factor to explain why the whole migration process came about. Conditions on the other side of the bridge—in the sender countries—must be taken into consideration.

The factors that explain why thousands of workers from all over Asia, given the demand, decided to leave their own labour markets to work on contract in the Gulf must be sought on different levels of analysis, as discussed in Chapter 1. The national economic situation and different institutional conditions provide a setting necessary for understanding the particular form and scale of the actual stream of migrants from each country.

Generally sender countries were highly eager to respond to the demand. Having little or no oil resources themselves, they were faced with the grim prospect of balance-of-payments deficits resulting from the international price rise on this essential commodity. The sender countries tried to compensate by encouraging their citizens to go abroad to work and subsequently to remit to the sender country as much as possible of their wages. In a number of countries such workers' remittances soon became the major foreign currency earner in the economy. Efforts to protect citizens from exploitation and various abuses by recruiting agents or employers in the Middle East has for the most part come as a secondary concern (Owen, 1986). Worries about possible adverse long-term effects of migration on the national economy have also been virtually nonexistent.

Sri Lanka is no exception to this general Asian picture. Concretely, the adoption of an export-oriented strategy of industrialization with the change of government in 1977 probably provides a central background for understanding the initiation of the migrant flow. Also important here was the deteriorating trend in the standard of living for the poorest sections of Sri Lankan society, starting in the 1970s.

The Political Economy of Sri Lanka After 1977

In many respects Sri Lanka appears to be a rather well-developed country; yet at the same time it is very poor, ranking among the thirty poorest countries in the world (per capita GNP at $360 in 1984). The Sri Lankan economy is, and has long been, closely integrated into the global economy. In 1985 the value of imports and exports together amounted to nearly 60% of GNP (Sørbø et al., 1987). The economy itself is relatively sophisticated, with market relations permeating all sectors, including small-scale farming. Even in the remotest parts of the rural sector, noncash economic transactions are rare.

It is the history of Sri Lanka, as a former colonial export economy under British rule (specializing in tea, rubber and coconuts) that largely explains the sophisticated economy as well as the fairly well-developed infrastructure. The export economy also explains the relatively high standard of living of the general population, as substantial export and import taxes have financed a welfare state of significance in the Third World context. Generally speaking, all governments in recent Sri Lankan history have been highly dependent on revenues extracted from the plantation sector. By 1947 there existed a network of free health and education services and a food ration system providing subsidised rice to almost the whole population.[1]

Since the late 1950s Sri Lanka has faced continuous balance-of-payments problems. In response to this condition, successive governments have introduced exchange and import controls as well as measures to direct investments towards import substitution. At the same time, the various governments have tried to maintain the system of social welfare. The measures have, in general, failed to resolve the basic balance-of-payment problems, improve economic growth and reduce unemployment.

Between 1970 and 1977 Sri Lanka was governed by a coalition, the United Front, with the Sri Lanka Freedom Party (SLFP) as the numerically dominant component. The other partners in the government—the Marxist Lanka Sama Samaj Party and the Communist Party—had a radicalizing influence on policies. The extent of state involvement in the economy was substantially expanded. State control was imposed on international trade and private access to foreign exchange; many private enterprises were nationalized, together with the whole plantation sector; new state production and trading corporations were initiated; and public sector employment was expanded rapidly.

Although there are different interpretations of the economic performance of this 1970–77 government, there seems to be little doubt that the overall economic situation was poor compared to both earlier and later periods—the average rate of GNP growth being less than 3%, compared to about 6% in the period since 1977. The general picture showed economic stagnation, increased unemployment and various scarcities, including food. Infant mortality rates increased significantly during this period (Sørbø, 1987).

Owing to the bad performance of the United Front government in the 1970s, the electorate responded by giving the opposition, the United National Party (UNP) a landslide victory at general elections in 1977. The UNP took 83% of the parliamentary seats at this event. The victory was achieved on a programme of economic liberalization. This package represented a fundamental policy change, aimed at transforming the Sri Lankan economy entirely. The most significant change was the shift from an inward-looking, fairly closed and controlled economy to an outward-looking policy with heavy market orientation.

Five major components can be traced from the new liberalization programme of the UNP government since 1977 (Sørbø, 1987):

1. The control system on private economic activity has been dismantled, in the sense that restrictions on business activities have been removed. Foreign trade is open to the private sector, and previous ceilings on ownership of residential property and agricultural land have been abolished.

2. Previous state monopolies have been opened up to private competition in the fields of consumer and producer services,

for example, in passenger-bus services, postal and telecommunication services (at the retail level), supplying of agricultural fertilisers, purchase of rice from farmers and rice milling.

3. The scope of public sector manufacturing has been reduced by a programme of privatization that includes the partial or complete sale of public corporations, the leasing of facilities on management contracts to the private sector and the closure of inefficient units and corporations.

4. Foreign private investment has been encouraged by the creation of free trade zones/export processing zones, along with the provision of tax incentives for foreign businesses entering into joint ventures with local capital outside the free trade zone.

5. There has been a major attempt to readjust prices by reducing the rate of state intervention in the price-setting and by letting the market determine the level in different sectors. Price controls have been abolished and subsidies have been phased out to allow the market mechanism to function smoothly and to facilitate a more efficient allocation of resources for productive purposes. Such a policy is also in line with the government's attempt to shift resources from consumption to investment.

Although the new government has clearly changed the economic policy of the country significantly through the 1977 liberalization programme, there are also important continuities from the previous period. Some of these features can be attributed to imminent contradictions in the new economic policy itself, and some can be traced back to distinct features of Sri Lankan society and polity in general.

In the first place, the whole new policy has from the beginning been heavily dependent on external economic support channelled mainly through the public sector. Since the introduction of the new policy, the Sri Lankan economy has been spending one-fifth more goods and services than it produces. This gap has been filled by foreign aid and commercial borrowing (Sørbø, 1987). The new government has initiated large public investment programmes like the Mahaweli power irrigation project, a major urban development scheme in Colombo and a national housing scheme, as well as provision of physical infrastructure for the new export processing zones. Ironically the objective of expanding the private sector and generally liberalizing the economy has required a heavy growth in the state sector to facilitate this expansion.[2]

In the second place, the parliamentary tradition and the "welfarist" state have created a political reality in which any government is obliged to meet some of the expectations of the population as to material living standard if it is to stay in power. The degree of ideological support for competitive capitalism seems very low in Sri Lanka, if it also involves neglecting the provision of welfare (Sørbø, 1987).

Consequently the real policy of the post-1977 government has been a balance of continuity and change in economic model: The economic reforms of Sri Lanka introduced in late 1977 have been a mixture of both conventional adjustment policies and policies influenced by sociopolitical considerations.

By and large, economic performance after 1977 has been better than that of the previous governmental period, as mentioned: GDP growth rates doubled in real terms, averaging over 6% per year during 1978–84, compared to an annual average of 2.9% in 1970–77. The reasons for this increase could be many, and a clear picture is difficult to draw, owing mainly to lack of accurate data. Foreign financial support has been mentioned and is probably one of the central factors. Domestic agriculture has also made an important contribution in this context. This sector grew by about 5%, mainly the result of substantial improvements in paddy production, which enabled the country to come close to self-sufficiency in rice. Until the ethnic conflict escalated in 1983, the tourist sector also showed promising results.

Probably even more important than tourism, though, has been the migration of Sri Lankans for employment in the Gulf. Earnings from this source are the dominant component of private remittances into Sri Lanka. These remittances have grown rapidly since the traffic commenced in 1976. Until 1975 more money was transferred out of the country than into it. With the labour migration, however, this situation changed such that in 1978 net private transfer financed 15% of the deficit on current payments for goods and services. The figure was 27% by 1982 and reached a peak of 56% in 1984. Put differently, by 1985 the value of net private transfers was equivalent to 60% of the value of tea exports (Sørbø, 1987).

National savings have also been greatly assisted by these foreign remittances; the domestic savings ratio, which was below 13% during 1970–77 had risen to 23% by 1984. The inflow of foreign exchange amounted to approximately US$280 million, or more than Rs 7 billion in 1984. This economic field has become even more important after the 1983 ethnic riots and the subsequent civil war, as the economy has become constrained concerning both tourism and foreign investment in general.

We have now looked briefly at the macroeconomic performance of the Sri Lankan state after 1977. What, then, have these different elements of the new policy programme meant in practice for the Sri Lankan population?

Inflation and Unemployment

Price increases were small prior to 1977, as inflationary pressures were by and large suppressed by price controls and rationing.[3] With the new economic policy after 1977 this picture changed completely. As changes in prices impact on real incomes, this field is relevant to any analysis of the effects of the new policy on different groups of the population.

It is evident that the price increases have been particularly high in basic commodities, especially food. This affects adversely the real incomes of lower income groups, relatively speaking, as purchases of these basic commodities constitute a large proportion of expenditure by these groups. Most strongly felt has been the price of basic foods like rice, wheat flour, bread and sugar. The price of rice increased by 158%, wheat flour by 386%, bread by 339% and milk powder by 345% between 1977 and 1984. These are the highest price increases of any commodity except for the price of kerosene, which increased by more than 700% in the same period.

Figure 3.1 shows that the price of food items rose by nearly 200%, fuel and light by nearly 400% and miscellaneous items (including medicines) by 138% between 1977 and 1984.

In the same period wage changes did not nearly compensate for these drastic price rises. However, the deterioration in real wages in the informal sector has been less than in the organized sector, because of the fairly fixed level of the wages in the latter.

Concerning employment the picture is more complex. A central aspect of the new economic policy was to increase employment. The Mahaweli project, the Urban Renewal Programme,

FIGURE 3.1 Price Increases, 1977–1984

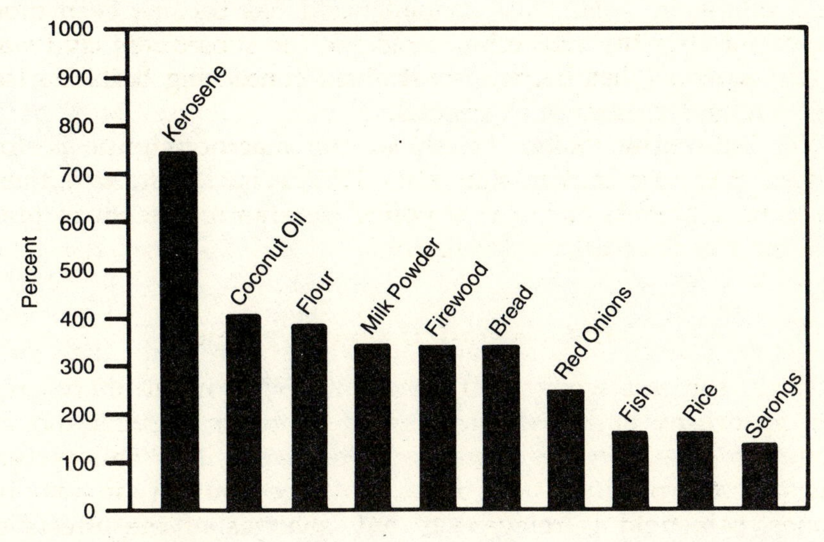

Source: Unicef, 1985.

and the Free Trade Zones were expected to generate new employment opportunities. The very high unemployment rates of the 1970s were believed to be the main reason behind the unrest that existed, particularly among youth. Although strong uncertainties are attached to measuring employment in general (particularly in economies dominated by the informal sector), there are indications that the rate of employment rose significantly from 1977 to 1983 (by approximately 24%, according to some figures). New opportunities were seen mostly in the rural sector, as well as in large numbers of small private enterprises.

Despite these improvements, however, unemployment remains a major problem in the economy, particularly in view of the rapid population increase. Even though overall unemployment has been reduced, unemployment among youth—particularly those with secondary education—is serious. In the period under consideration unemployment decreased in all age groups except the age group of 14–18 years, where it remained more or less static at 31%. For the age group of 19–25 years the rate was still approximately 28% in 1987.

Welfare and the Standard of Living

During the 1970s the food subsidy system formed one of the cornerstones of Sri Lanka's welfare policy towards large parts of the population. After the shift of government in 1977 this system was reformed substantially, with significant effects on the standard of living of the poorer sections of the population. Basically two reforms took place in 1978–79. First, the food subsidy was withdrawn from approximately one-half of the households, based on estimates of household income. According to the authorities, this act was undertaken to remedy the worst flaws of the existing system, which was believed to be highly inefficient and not reaching all of the target groups. After the transformation of the system, the new list of households eligible for food subsidies was fixed, meaning that no adjustments could be made for households that became poor. Second, the previous subsidy system for food, supplied in terms of rations of food (mainly rice) per person per week, was replaced by a food stamp of a fixed monetary value. This monetary value did not change between 1979 and 1986 despite the high rate of inflation in the same period. It is estimated that the real value of the food stamp fell by at least 60% between 1979 and 1986 (the cost of food subsidies fell from 11% to 2% of all government expenditures between 1979 and 1985) (Sørbø, 1987).

Although drawing an aggregate picture of this welfare situation is difficult, the reforms of the food subsidy programme are seen to have affected the poorest sections of society significantly after 1979. The group most adversely effected may comprise some 10–15% of all households in the country (Sørbø, 1987:47). The new system removed the security of the guaranteed minimum consumption level that had been provided by the previous free rice ration. Among the lowest-income groups consumption levels fell as low as 1,181 calories per person per day in 1981–82.

The trend towards greater equality in income distribution evident in the period from 1953 to 1973 was stopped in 1978–79 and 1981–82 (according to the Consumer Finance Survey of this period). The overall distribution of income over time has become considerably less equal, but available data do not reveal clearly whether the deterioration has been any stronger under the post-1977 government than it was during the 1970s. Neither period has generated any marked improvement in the standard of living among the poorest or in income distribution (Sørbø, 1987).[4]

Notes

1. There are important exceptions within this favourable picture of a "welfare state." Subsections of society, and particularly women, among the plantation Tamils and the Muslim population in the eastern part of the island were not reached by the welfare measures to the same extent as the rest of the population. (See, e.g., Moore, 1985; and Jayawardene and Jayaweera, 1985.) These qualifications will be treated later in the book.

2. This situation is not at all unique to Sri Lanka. It seems to be a basic contradiction for poor countries adopting ideals of economic liberalism that they can take the risk only if they are heavily supported from abroad. This support, in turn, usually has to be negotiated and administered through the state machinery (Moore, 1985; Sørbø, 1987).

3. Most of the data in this section are quoted from unpublished material from a research project conducted by the World Bank and the Central Bank of Sri Lanka, "The evolution of the living standards in Sri Lanka," and some unpublished material from UNICEF, Colombo.

4. The difficulties of getting a clear picture from the available data is discussed in more detail in Sørbø (1987: 205–214).

4

The Migration Connection

Because we know that it is from the poorest section of society that the clear majority of female migrants are recruited, it is appropriate to relate this phenomenon to tendencies in the national economy in the period prior to the exodus and in the period during which migration developed into a major element of the national economic scenario.[1]

Initiation of the Traffic

We have seen that the standard of living of the lower strata of the population has deteriorated significantly since the early 1970s. We have also seen that the post-1977 government faced a set of problems after having introduced the new economic policy of export industrialization: a very high rate of inflation, a sizable hard currency deficit and increasing youth unemployment.

The increased demand for labour in the Gulf gave the Sri Lankan government a means to remedy some of its worst economic problems by providing hard currency while also alleviating unemployment among certain groups of the people. Furthermore, it also gave individual households a way not only of compensating for the deterioration of their standard of living but of gaining a new and fairly lucrative source of income.

The exodus of skilled and unskilled labour to the Middle East commenced about 1975 on a small-scale basis and increased rapidly after 1978. We have seen how the labour-importing countries, for different reasons, started diversifying their sources of labour recruitment after the oil boom started. Sri Lankans represented an attractive alternative in many respects. Wage differentials between the Gulf countries and Sri Lanka were high, so that labour power could be sold at a comparatively low price. Close proximity to the region, and thereby lower travel expenses, was an additional advantage. The liberalized economic policies of the Sri Lankan government actually encouraged the flow of labour out of the country, and consequently enabled migrants to process their travel documents fairly efficiently (Korale, 1985b).

Since the late 1970s the total flow of migrants from Sri Lanka to the Middle East has increased steadily. By 1985 some 250,000 to 300,000 families, or about one-tenth of the total population of Sri Lanka, had been directly involved through having a family member who had worked or was working abroad (Economic Review, 1985).[2] Migrant remittances have become the second largest source of foreign exchange to the country, after the traditional tea export (Korale et al., 1985).

At first only men went as labourers to the Gulf, and most of them were absorbed in government service, municipalities, public corporations, multinational firms and small private sector trading (Korale, 1985b:51). From the late 1970s and early 1980s, however, women also started going on contracts, predominantly as private housemaids. The share of female migrants of the total has increased steadily, comprising 47% in 1979, 53% in 1981, and approximately 57% by 1985 (Korale et al., 1985). Since 1985 this tendency has been reinforced, as relatively fewer men are recruited, in line with the policy of Arabization of main sectors of the Gulf economies.[3]

These women had the same basic advantages as the Sri Lankan men concerning proximity and wage differentials (Sri Lanka actually advertised itself internationally as having the "cheapest labour power in Asia"). Additionally, the country had a comparative advantage in the region, as most other sender countries—Pakistan, Bangladesh, Indonesia and, to a certain extent, India—had imposed restrictions on the export of female labour power for cultural and religious reasons. In consequence, Sri Lanka acquired almost a monopoly position from the beginning.

This fact does not make it any less striking in the Sri Lankan context that thousands of women fairly quickly responded to the radical option of leaving their homes and local communities to take a two-year job in a foreign country.[4] Moreover, most of these women were married, often with very young children. Job arrangements in the Middle East do not permit other family members of these women to come along, so migrants are virtually cut off from direct contact with their spouses and children for two-year periods. The combination of these social factors and the contract character of the work is in essence what makes the Sri Lankan case special on the international scene.

There are several forceful aspects of this phenomenon when it comes to the cultural traditions and values in the country, which have provided women with a fairly restrictive set of options concerning activities outside the household. Lack of mobility, with reference to the need for protection has been one of the most salient features of women's possibilities outside the home sphere in Sri Lanka (see Chapter 6). The great majority of these women migrants have accordingly never had any paid job prior to migration (Korale et al., 1985). Taking up employment in the Gulf consequently represents a radical decision on many dimensions, although it becomes less radical with time and with larger numbers of people making the same decision.

Since the traffic started, stories have circulated about the various difficulties awaiting the women overseas, spread both through newspapers and through direct communication with returnees in the local communities. Hardly any Sri Lankan woman would leave without knowing that the possibilities of running into serious trouble are fairly high. She might be cheated economically at different stages in the migration process or be maltreated in the households (including sexual abuse by the employer), and she might not stand the psychological pressure of being placed in a completely strange environment, often cut off from contact with the outside world. Yet even though they have heard of these risks, Sri Lankan women keep queuing up to go overseas. This fact probably reflects the gravity of their social and economic problems at home, as well as the highly favourable wage conditions in the Gulf relative to the situation in Sri Lanka.

The wage differential between the Gulf and the national labour market for these groups of people is approximately 10 to 1. Moreover, most female migrants (and potential migrants) would not have even the possibility of getting a paid job at home. Maids' salaries are also much higher than what their men can hope for in the national labour market—if they get any employment at all. Consequently the offer from the Gulf is in many cases the only option for the families involved, and any other available alternatives can hardly compete with wage levels in the Gulf. This wage differential is unquestionably the single strongest pull factor in the situation.

Institutions in Migration Promotion

Since the option of sending labour power abroad on a large scale has presented itself as extremely favourable to the Sri Lankan government in the post-1977 period, the question of promotion and organization has been central. As no government-to-government arrangement or agreement between Sri Lanka and the Arab states existed, and as the Sri Lankan state apparatus itself could not possibly take up the task of recruiting labour, foreign employment agencies played an important role from the outset of the traffic. The government encouraged the private sector, and a large number of firms that had been engaged in unrelated activities but had experience in international trade and commerce were granted licences as recruitment agencies. These agents established contact with counterparts in the Gulf area that acted as intermediaries to the prospective employers (Korale, 1985b:34). The comprehensive engagement of private agencies has heavily influenced the size, composition and growth of Sri Lankan migration to the Middle East. It has also contributed to making such recruitment a business and thereby had a significant impact on the way money is channelled through the system and on the extent to which the labourer herself/himself profits from the contract.

The first few private agencies were established in 1975, and the Foreign Employment Division of the Department of Labour, which was established in 1976, was given the function of supervising and regulating the work of these agencies. Foreign employment agencies were registered under the provisions of the Fee Charging Employment Agency Act no. 37 of 1956. By the end of 1978 125 agencies had registered with the Department of Labour, a number that increased rapidly to 525 by the end of 1980 with the increasing demand for Sri Lankan labour.

Owing to this strong demand and the business aspects of the traffic, a plethora of unregistered agencies cropped up throughout the country. In order to control the malpractices committed by these agencies, the government tried to establish formal provisions to "safeguard the rights of job seekers and prospective migrants" (Korale et al., 1985:17). The result was the enactment of the Foreign Employment Agency Act no. 37 of 1980, which required agencies to register with the Department of Labour. By the beginning of 1984 400 agents had followed this rule. To further control the Middle East traffic in terms of recruitment and minimum standards for wages, hours of work and holidays for workers going abroad, the Sri Lanka Bureau of Foreign Employment was established in 1985 (Act no. 21) (Marga, 1986).

Sri Lankan embassies have also been established in some of the recipient countries (UAE, Saudi Arabia, Kuwait, Lebanon and Iraq), with a labour officer attached whose particular function is to be concerned with the Sri Lankan migrants. These diplomatic missions will, however, "not interfere in any issues pertaining to the status of the migrants in the Middle East" (Sarath, 1984). The migration question is a delicate diplomatic issue, and the Sri Lankan authorities probably have to consider the political effect of possible interventions. In view of the economic conditions of the country the authorities can scarcely afford to lose their share of the lucrative, albeit now increasingly competitive, Middle East labour market. In addition, there are practical problems involved in supervising the maids, particularly as they are widely dispersed and often distant from the diplomatic centres.[5]

Despite efforts made by the Sri Lankan government to maintain the upper hand with the recruitment of labour to the Middle East, bureaucratic control over local unregistered agents has been virtually nil throughout the period. The number of migrants who obtain employment through unregistered agencies is and has been significantly higher than the numbers placed by the licensed ones. According to available estimates only one-third of the total stock of migrants are placed by registered agents. Almost every town has at least one unlicensed agent (Korale et al., 1985).

There could be many reasons for this uncontrolled mushrooming of illegal recruitment agencies. Prospective migrants are usually so anxious to secure jobs abroad that it is highly unlikely that they would report illegal agents, even when they are forced to pay many times the legal fee. Even more important is probably the fact that most people are not aware of official recruitment policies and would consequently not be familiar with the legal level of fees nor in a position to verify that their agent was registered. Experience from other sender countries also indicates that it is virtually impossible to keep recruitment from flourishing when there is a buoyant job market overseas.

The uncontrolled recruitment situation is nevertheless a major factor in the class-related composition and effects of the Middle East labour traffic. The maximum legal fee for the agencies, according to the Act no. 21 of 1985, is Rs 2,700 (US$1 = Rs 44). In reality, the unregistered agents charge several times more—up to Rs 9,000 for maids. Fees are higher for men (sometimes as high as Rs 55,000), as their salaries in the Gulf are also much higher. According to the Leiden-Colombo Survey (Eelens, Schampers and Speckmann, 1992), recruitment fees have increased in the first half of the 1980s at an average rate of about 2% per month. On the average, housemaids had to pay Rs 826 in the early 1980s. By 1986 the average had increased to Rs 4,314. Since they are in demand, Muslims (Moors and Malays) can manage to leave at cheaper rates. On the average they pay 13% and 32% less, respectively, than do Sinhalese.

These highly priced entry tickets to jobs in the Middle East certainly reduce the net value of the contracts for the migrants themselves, particularly for those from poor backgrounds. Lacking capital to pay the fee, these migrants consequently have to borrow money at high interest rates. This is indeed the case for a high number of the female migrants.

Another factor has increased the economic burden on migrants in the chain of operators in the system. Competition among sender countries has become stiffer since the process of Arabization started in the Gulf. Diminishing employment opportunities have made agencies undercut each other, often not charging a commission from the agents on the receiver side and thus having to recover the entire cost of recruitment from the migrant herself/himself (Korale et al., 1985:34).

Selection Procedure

When a prospective client contacts a recruiter, an interview is undertaken during which an application form is filled in. The interview is often conducted in English, partly to test the language skills of the client. In practice this often means that hardly anything is grasped by the prospective maid. The agents frequently take care of the passport application as well, which increases their control. Often the client has to pay a sum of money in advance, adding heavy costs if this money has to be borrowed.

Just before departure a compulsory health check is carried out. For housemaids it is essential to ensure that the migrant is not pregnant because pregnancy is one of the reasons she can be sent back home within three months of arrival—the probationary period fixed by contract. These early returns are charged to the recruitment agent. To avoid this possibility, the client is often injected with contraceptives (Eelens, Schampers and Speckmann, 1992).

Sometimes the client is also tested in relevant job skills. This practice is not common for housemaids, although other criteria play a part. In addition to religious affiliation, age is a factor. Minimum age varies depending on the country of destination: Kuwait and Bahrain require the client to be at least 18 years old; in Saudi Arabia the minimum age is 30. The maximum age is generally 35–40 years. Appearance, behaviour and family situation are also taken into consideration. When the employer in the Gulf chooses a maid, the photograph often plays an important part. Some figures also indicate that there are agents who prefer applicants from outside the city areas "because they are mostly accustomed to hard work and are supposed to be disciplined" (Eelens, Schampers and Speckmann, 1992). According to T. Mook (1992), some agents also believe that "spending rural women is more profitable, because they are more easily cheated than urban girls. The rural people will agree to pay vast sums of rupees—10,000 and more."

When the procedure has been completed on the Sri Lankan side, some instructions are given as to practicalities on the journey as well as some rules and regulations in the country of destination. The contract, usually signed just before departure, is in 84% of the cases drawn up in English and provides only a few details as to working conditions (Eelens, Schampers and Speckmann, 1992).

The desire to increase remittances from migrant traffic has determined much of the direction of official policy on this issue in Sri Lanka. Along with the growth in the traffic, strong vested interests have been created, not only at the state level but also in parts of the private sector such as airlines, banking and trade. Even though one should not doubt the official concern about all the irregularities and malpractices attached to the business at different levels, the overriding objective has been to keep the traffic going at the highest rate possible. This export of labour has been a central component in the development programme of the Sri Lankan government, particularly as it pertains to unskilled and semiskilled labour, where employment prospects within the national economy have not been bright. To this end the government has provided incentives and infrastructure—liberal rules for agencies; travel arrangements; passport provision; possibilities of importing foreign currency and opening private foreign currency accounts; and reintegration assistance, including courses for establishing private businesses after the return to Sri Lanka.[6] Thus the government aims at extracting as much revenue as possible out of the labour export without in practice being too occupied with either the possible adverse long-term effects on the economy or the social implications, particularly concerning the female contingent.

General Characteristics of Migrants

In this section the empirical findings based on interviews in both Colombo and Hambantota (totaling 140) in 1985–86 are presented to give an overall impression, that is, the general characteristics of the women who were interviewed in this study. Figures from Hambantota and Colombo are combined in the cases in which differences are insignificant. These data are further illustrated by findings from the two national surveys (Korale et al., 1985; Marga, 1986), which represent aggregated data from (in a formal sense) more representative samples, in order to present the concrete phenomenon in a broad sense, before we take up the two specific communities in more detail (Chapter 7).

Characteristics of Migrants and Migrants' Households

The outer age limits of the migrants seem to be 17 and 45 years. Since housework in the Middle East is physically and mentally demanding, there are some natural limits as to which age groups are in demand. Within this age range 66% of the sample were between 21 and 36 years old; 29% were 37 and above, and only 4% were 20 and below. This picture is backed up by the two national surveys (according to Marga, 1986, 96% of the women were in the age group 25–39).

The ethnic composition of the migrant group is of interest relative to the ongoing internal conflict between the Sri Lanka Tamils and the Sinhala majority. (The terms Sinhala and Sinhalese are used interchangeably.) Our sample, however, was not selected to provide any representative distribution of the various ethnic communities, as the different groups were not representatively distributed within the two major communities that were chosen. The pockets in Colombo were predominantly Sinhalese; in Hambantota, Muslim (Malay and Moor). Of the total migrant sample 70% were Sinhalese, 7% Tamil and 23% Muslim. National data show, however, that the percentage of the Tamil migrants is much less than their share in the total population. The reasons for this inconsistency would probably be different for the Sri Lanka Tamils in the north and in the east than for the Indian Tamils in the plantation areas in the middle of the country. Although labour migration could have been a convenient escape from a war situation for the Sri Lanka Tamils, the possibilities are scarce. There are proportionally fewer agents operating in the north and east, and travelling south has been difficult and insecure. The problem for the plantation Tamils, apart from the fact that they are fairly isolated from the rest of the population, is that they are still by and large not citizens of Sri Lanka and therefore are not entitled to passports. The Muslim population, however, is clearly overrepresented. The Sri Lankan Moors constitute only 7% of the inhabitants of Sri Lanka yet comprised 23% of the migrant group to the Middle East (both male and female; unfortunately there are no separate figures for the female component). The picture of the ethnic distribution is Sinhala, 66%; Sri Lanka Tamils, 7%; Indian Tamils, 0.2%; Moors, 23% (Korale et al., 1985). The pattern of religion largely follows ethnic distribution, as the correlation between ethnic group and creed is high. By and large, the Sinhala are Buddhists, Tamils are Hindu and Moors and Malays are Muslim. The small variation relates mainly to some Sinhalese and Tamils being Christians.

As Table 4.1 shows, the clear majority of the sample was married. The category "divorced" means "living alone after having been married," as very few people are formally divorced. The percentage who were married is even higher in the national samples: 71% (Marga, 1986) and 76% (Korale et al., 1985). Even though married women were in the majority, there is no clear indication of preference for married maids from the employers. Indeed, a number of job agents express a preference for unmarried girls from rural areas, as they are believed to work harder and complain less. Others, however, prefer married women because of their experience with housework and children (Eelens and Schampers, 1986).

Table 4.2 shows that 29% of the total sample had no children and that the majority of the migrants had between 1 and 4 children. A surprisingly high percentage (19) had 5 or more. This table reveals a high dependency ratio in the migrant households.

The size of the household is not necessarily related to number of children, as many households include people other than the core family, usually parents or other relatives. (See Table 4.3.) Particularly in relation to the migration, female relatives are drawn into the household to substitute for the migrant, even if they did not live there before. This is reflected in the fact that the great majority of the households in the sample consisted of 5–10 people. Korale et al. (1985) found that generally the size of the migrant households was larger (6.4) than the island average (5.5) for both male and female migrants.

The educational background of the migrants is fairly equally distributed under the A-level, with a slight majority having completed 5th grade or less. (See Table 4.4.) According to

TABLE 4.1 Marital Status of Female Migrants to the Gulf

Marital Status	*N*	%
Married	85	61
Unmarried	32	23
Divorced	18	13
Widowed	5	4
	140	101

TABLE 4.2 Number of Children of Female Migrants to the Gulf

Number of Children	*N*	%
0	41	29
1–2	42	30
3–4	31	22
5+	26	19
	140	100

TABLE 4.3 Size of Households of Female Migrants to the Gulf

Number in Household	*N*	%
2–4	42	30
5–7	61	44
8–10		14
11+		12
		100

TABLE 4.4 Educational Level Achieved by Female Migrants to the Gulf

Level Completed	*N*	%
>5 grade		35
5–7	43	31
8–O-level[a]		31
A-level +[b]	4	3
	140	100

[a]O=ordinary level (11 years)
[b]A=advanced level (3 additional years)

TABLE 4.5 Level of Household Income of Female Migrants Prior to Migration

Rupees (Rs)/month	*N*	%
0–500	45	32
501–800	39	28
801–1,500	33	24
1,500+	23	16
	140	100

Korale's data, 53% of the migrants had between 0 and 9 years of education; only 2% had no schooling at all. Although the quality of the education varies considerably throughout the country, the general level of education in Sri Lanka is high compared to that in other developing countries (see chapter 3). The average educational level of the migrants has a distribution somewhat different from the national female average, in which 62% had completed primary education (5–7 grade); 7%, O-levels, and 1%, A-levels (Census of Population, 1981). Of other members of the household 71% of the sample reported none with O-levels or more, 21% reported one and 9% reported more than one. Thus the general educational level of the migrant household was average or below average.

In response to the question whether the women had had paid work prior to the Middle East job, 79% reported no and 21% reported yes. According to the Marga data 70% of the women nationwide were reported to have been housewives. These figures can be misleading, as a number of women may have had some sort of paid work in their lives, consequently reporting yes even though the duration of the work could have been negligible. The clear impression is that 21% is too high a figure if by "paid work" one means anything lasting and fairly structured. According to Korale's data, 58% of the total sample had had no income whatsoever prior to migration.

Table 4.5 indicates that the majority of the households belong to the lower income strata. According to Korale et al. (1985), 58% of the sample reported having no income at all, and 76% had a monthly income of less than Rs 800. Since migrant households are comparatively large, such an income level is insufficient for most of them to subsist on. The majority of the households also reported having only one person earning any money before the Middle East departure. Accordingly, the reason for going was overwhelmingly stated to be financial (94%) (Marga: 96%). Although this is a relative statement, the impression was almost invariably consistent: The major motivation for going is basic economic problems.

Another factor that could influence the standard of living in the households is whether more than one person from the household is working in the Gulf. As can be seen from Table 4.6, this was the case for only a small portion of the sample.

TABLE 4.6 Other Family Members of Female Migrants also Working in the Gulf

Family Members	*N*	%
0–None	104	75
One sister	14	10
2 sisters/daughters	7	5
3 sisters	7	5
Brother/other	6	4
	138	99
		2 NI[a]

[a]NI = Not included

Conditions Related to the Contract

The following tables provide information about the conditions on which the migrants establish (and possibly break) their contracts.

At the time of the interviews, 62% of the returned migrants reported having been in the Gulf only once, 32% had been there twice and 6% three times. However, 80% of the sample stated that they would like to go again if the possibility arose. Many also had concrete plans for going on a new contract. Within several years, therefore, the number of women who report having been abroad more than once will probably be higher. Of those interviewed, 16% reported that they had been in the same household in the Gulf more than once. If arrangements for repeating employment are worked out directly with the household, the migrant will not have to bear the expense of an agent, and adjustment problems are likely to be reduced.

The number of times a migrant has gone to the Middle East was not, however, necessarily identical to the number of completed contracts (full two-year periods). Of the women reporting, 38% had broken the contract once and 4% twice. (Korale shows that 15% of the female migrants stay less than six months. The average stay for all women is one year, five months.)

The majority of the migrants (64% of the sample) obtained a work contract through a recruitment agency (Korale's figure is 55%, although it reflects only registered agencies, a small part of the whole group of agents). This high percentage also implies that many migrants have a fairly high level of expense attached to establishing a contract.

Among the various ethnic groups, there was a significant difference between Sinhalese and Muslim migrants, on the one hand, and Tamils, on the other, concerning propensity to pay agent fees. (See Table 4.7.) Of the Tamils 50% paid between Rs 3,001 and Rs 6,000 compared to 7% and 16% among Sinhala and Muslim migrants, respectively. (A weakness of this figure is that the basis for calculation concerning the Tamil group is small compared to the others.)

The agent fee, however, is only one of many expenses the migrants have in relation to the Middle East migration. Other expenses include the cost of processing travel documents, a medical fitness test, travelling and subsistence related to travelling, equipment and personal effects and bribes to possible middlemen. The other costs can vary substantially from case to case, depending on where in the country the migrant lives, among other factors. Many migrants have to travel to Colombo several times to deal with the various formalities of establishing a contract. By and large, however, the agent fee is the greatest expense. Table 4.8 shows that among the migrants from Hambantota 82% of the sample spend Rs 1,000 or more on other expenses, whereas the figure for Colombo is only 36%.

Also important concerning the establishment of a contract is how much the migrant household has to borrow in order to go. We note (Table 4.9) that the largest group within the sample (40%) had borrowed money to cover the various expenses at an interest rate of 20% per month. This figure is significant and underlines the serious economic burden for many migrant households attached to establishing a contract. The Marga data reveal in this context that more women than men have to borrow money to go abroad, probably because female migrants are poorer than male migrants, and that they consequently lack access to other sources of money (richer relatives and friends or adequate property for mortgage or sale). It is suggested that this is the case, even though male migrants have to pay a much higher agent fee than women do.

Three Stages in the Migration Process

I have so far discussed the interlinkages between the sending and the receiving ends of the migration connection as a background for understanding processes on lower levels of analysis.

TABLE 4.7 Propensity of Female Migrants to Pay Agent Fee, by Ethnic Group

	Fee (in Rs)						
Group	*0*	*0–1,000*	*1,001–3,000*	*3,001–6,000*	*6,001+*	*%*	*N*
Sinhala	56	14	18	7	4	101	98
Tamil	0	20	30	50	0	100	10
Muslim	47	22	13	16	3	101	32
%	50	16	18	12	4	100	
N	70	23	25	17	5		140

TABLE 4.8 Other Costs to Female Migrants of Obtaining a Gulf Contract, Controlled for Area

Costs (Rs)	*Colombo*	*Hambantota*	*Total %*	*N*
0–500		26	4	30
501–1,000		38	15	46
1,001+	36	82	45	63
Total %	100	101	100	
N	111	27		139 1 NI

TABLE 4.9 Method of Raising Money to Cover Expenses of a Gulf Contract

	N	*%*
No costs	3	2
Saved money	18	13
Loan with no interest	26	19
Loan with <20% interest	23	17
Loan with 20% interest	55	40
Pawned things	13	9
	138	100 2 NI

I have noted the situation in the Gulf—the oil price boom of the early 1970s—as a necessary but not sufficient precondition for the development of labour migration from Asia to the Middle East. The internal dilemmas attached to basing development of the national economies on imported labour on the pull side have also been touched upon to enable us to appraise future prospects for the migration stream.

I have also discussed central aspects of the Sri Lankan side, namely, important changes in the national economy that have adversely affected the poorer sections of society, the very groups from which female migrant workers are recruited. The suggestion is that deteriorating social and economic conditions in Sri Lanka constitute a relevant background for understanding the phenomenon of labour migration to the Middle East from the mid-1970s onwards. A precondition for this option was the development taking place in the Gulf. To effectuate a push, there has to be a pull.

Furthermore, the concrete decisions of individuals on the local level are influenced by other important contextual factors pertaining to cultural norms, values and roles. (These aspects are discussed in Chapters 5, 7, and 8. In this chapter I have discussed possible explanatory variables for why the traffic came about and how the sum of the individual migrants, through their action, have influenced the national economy of Sri Lanka.

Future prospects of the labour traffic to the Middle East are contingent on a number of factors, both in Sri Lanka and in the Gulf states themselves. Possibly the pull side will become a push side, closing the borders to foreign labour and thereby compelling the original push area to become a pull area. There are problems on both sides if the migration stream continues to flow and problems if it is stopped. So far on the Sri Lankan side, I have discussed only the incentives on the state level. In Chapter 8 the more problematic aspects, both for the households and for the country as a whole, will be dealt with.

It is useful to differentiate between stages—in time and space—in the total migration process, to sort out which specific forces are in motion at each step for the individual migrant. Three major stages may be singled out: (1) the initial premigration stage in Sri Lanka, (2) the period in the Gulf and (3) the postmigration stage back in the home community. Within each stage there are a diversity of variables that in combination form the total outcome or net result of the individual migrant's work experience.

Sri Lanka Before Leaving: Initial Resources. Different households have different *initial resources* before the contract is signed, that is, they live under different social and economic conditions from the outset in a broad sense. The kind of economy that constitutes the basis for the household, independent of the Gulf money, is of importance, as is the demographic composition of the household: At what stage of the life cycle are the different members? How many members need support? The degree of indebtedness of the household and the network resources as well as the general set of resources like health, education and kind/degree of household organisation are also significant variables. All these factors are likely to interact and influence the possibilities to make efficient use of the income from the Middle East.

In the Gulf: Process Conditions. The stay in the Gulf will to a varying degree be successful for the women, depending on the following factors: the degree to which they are swindled by the recruiting agent and/or the employer, that is, whether they receive the salary in accordance with the contract; what the working conditions are like; to what degree they endure physical or psychological pressure; whether they are called home because of illness or other problems in the family; and to what degree they are victims of other misfortunes.

All of these process conditions are of importance in determining the value of the stay. It is also likely that the initial resources of the group of women who actually go interact with the process conditions, in the sense that their individual resources influence the way they are treated and the way they react to the treatment.

After Returning to Sri Lanka: Dispositional Effects. The third factor that influences the end result concerns how the money is used. The administration of the regularly remitted money is likely to be of major importance for the more lasting gains of the household. Given the fact that the household's standard of living from the outset is low, marginal differences in planning and administration will probably have a significant impact. Whether the money is used in a controlled way, is invested or possibly saved or is squandered or spent casually is obviously an essential factor. Central questions in this respect are the following: How are the remittances handled while the woman is away? Are they sent home during the course of the stay and, if so, to whom are they sent? How is the money spent, and to what extent does the woman have any influence on the disposition? As a consequence of the disposition of the remittances, have the remittances had any lasting impact on the household economy? To what extent have remittances had any impact on the social position of the woman, on the one hand, and her household, on the other? Have experiences from the first trip abroad had any impact on the disposition of the woman's remittances during a possible second (or third) stay?

We assume that conditions related to these three clusters of variables interact to determine what each household and individual woman get out of a contract in the Middle East. When the traffic has been going on for a while, information from the work sphere in the Gulf affects decisionmaking at home. Actual experiences from earlier contracts (in all stages) will also influence the individual's further relations to the migration chain.

In Chapters 5 and 6 I present data related to the different stages—both background data and more specific findings from this study. First, the position of women in the Sri Lankan society (stage 1) is analyzed and described, and second, the conditions of the housemaids in the Gulf (stage 2) are discussed. Chapter 5 presents the cultural and economic setting in which the Sri Lankan women act. It serves to shed light on the motivational side: the circumstances that can explain why the women started leaving their traditional niche. Chapter 6 presents the work setting, which is more or less realistically communicated to the prospective migrant women in Sri Lanka and thereby represents one of the premises for decisionmaking. The effect side will be handled in Chapter 7.

Notes

1. The class aspect of female migration from Sri Lanka has been scrutinized in various contexts, the most substantial ones being the two surveys undertaken by the Marga Institute and the Ministry of Plan Implementation (Marga, 1986; Korale et al., 1985). These two surveys represent the only comprehensive data sources (with their weaknesses) that are available in addition to the recent survey undertaken by the joint Colombo-Leiden research team (Eelens, Schampers and Speckmann, 1990).

2. Figures are generally uncertain concerning labour migration from Sri Lanka, as registration is limited. There are reasons to believe that the official estimates are too low concerning all types of labour exports. Estimates indicate that about 150,000 Sri Lankan women were working in the Gulf in 1986 (Eelens and Schampers, 1988).

3. Calculations in the late 1980s indicate that about 70% of the Sri Lankan migrants were women (Eelens and Schampers, 1988). According to the Sri Lankan ambassador in Kuwait, between 50,000 and 60,000 Sri Lankan housemaids were working in that country alone.

4. Cultural and other significant aspects will be treated in Chapter 5. The more factual sides are stressed in this chapter.

5. Nevertheless, between 1978 and 1982 these diplomatic missions received 2,400 complaints about unsatisfactory working and living conditions in the Middle East; most of them came from the housemaids (*Voice of Women,* 1982).

6. This has applied only to male migrants so far.

5

Status of Women in Sri Lanka

I have so far dealt with gender issues in a rather general and theoretical manner. In this chapter the more concrete setting of women's status in Sri Lanka will be discussed. The purpose is to provide a context in which to place female Sri Lankan employment in the Middle East in terms of economy, politics and culture.

Historical processes are important for understanding how dominant ideologies concerning sex roles and women's status interact with economic factors to bring about the structuring of very specific social spaces for women. I begin with a brief look into the past regarding the interconnected issues of women in relation to work and dominant social norms in society.

Some Statistical Facts

The figures presented so far about Sri Lanka's socioeconomic setting (Chapter 3) have been gender neutral. A picture was drawn (although with important qualifications) of a developing country with significantly high scores on central social and economic indicators during the 1970s, followed by a period of recession with particularly negative effects on lower social strata after 1977. Statistically speaking, this general picture also applies to the women of the island. As Tables 5.1, 5.2 and 5.3 show, Sri Lankan women have an average life expectancy of 67 years, a literacy rate of 82% and a maternal mortality rate of only 1.2 per thousand births. These figures are strikingly favorable compared with most Third World countries and even with some countries of the developed world. The figures also show that women compare favorably with Sri Lankan men in life expectancy and literacy rates.

TABLE 5.1 Trends in Life Expectancy at Birth, by Sex, and Rapidity of Mortality Decline, by Sex and Stage, 1921–1971

	Expectation of Life at Birth	
Year	*Male*	*Female*
1921	32.6	30.6
1946	43.8	41.5
1953	57.8	55.7
1963	62.8	63.0
1971	64.0	66.9

Source: Registrar-General's Reports on Vital Statistics, 1921–1971, Sri Lanka (Ceylon).

TABLE 5.2 Percentage of Literates

Year	*Females*	*All Island*
1881	3.1	17.4
1911	12.5	31.0
1921	21.2	39.9
1946	43.8	57.8
1963	63.2	71.6
1971	70.9	78.5
1981	82.8	86.5

Source: Census Reports, 1881, 1891, 1921, 1946, 1963, 1971, 1981, Sri Lanka (Ceylon).

TABLE 5.3 Maternal Death Rates, 1921–1974

Year	*Maternal Death Rate*
1921–1930	19.8
1931–1940	20.1
1941–1950	12.0
1951–1960	4.4
1961–1970	2.2
1971	1.2
1972	1.2
1973	1.2
1974	1.2

Source: Registrar-General's Reports on Vital Statistics, 1921–1974, Sri Lanka (Ceylon).

As usual, though, figures like these show only aggregates, which means that they do not reveal whether the population has benefited equally. If we break down the figures by region and ethnicity, significant variation emerges: Some underdeveloped and remote areas of the island show much worse welfare conditions compared to the urban areas. One group that has always been relatively deprived in a national context is plantation labour, with standards below average in both health and education. Muslim groups on the Eastern coast of Sri Lanka and landless rural labour and urban slum dwellers are other significant deprived groups.

For our purposes, however, what is more relevant is the gender bias in the figures. Statistics available for some sectors show a marked discrepancy between the sexes, particularly in the plantation sector. (See Tables 5.4 and 5.5.) It appears that even among those groups that are relatively deprived, women are worse off than men (Jayawardene and Jayaweera, 1985). Thus whereas the national literacy level for women is 83%, it is only 57% among the female plantation workers (estate sector).[1] (See Table 5.6).

These figures indicate that sex is an important variable on top of class position when it comes to the general welfare situation of the population. Nevertheless, women have shared in the improvement of the physical quality of life that has taken place in Sri Lanka since independence in 1948. This favorable situation relative to that of women in other Third World countries does not necessarily imply, however, that the subordination of women has decreased along with the physical advancement. There are strong indications that the basic subordinate position of women in Sri Lankan society has not changed significantly during the same period (see University of Colombo, 1979; and CENWOR, 1985).

Identity of Woman: Ethnicity and Caste

Being a multiethnic society, Sri Lanka (Ceylon) used to be governed by different customary laws according to religion and ethnicity. The most important functioning laws up to the last colonial period were the traditional Sinhalese law, the customary law of the Kandyan region, the Thesavalamai or Hindu

TABLE 5.4 Infant Mortality in Estate and Non-estate Areas, Selected Years (deaths per 1,000 live births)

Year	*Estate*	*Non-estate*	*Non-estate as percent of Estate*
1930	194	172	89
1940	149	149	100
1950	108	79	73
1955	115	66	57
1960	100	52	52
1965	94	49	52
1971	93	41	44
1973	103	42	41
1974	163	43	26
1975	102	41	40
1976	110	n.a.	n.a.

Source: S. A. Meegama, "Socio-economic Determinants of Infant and Child Mortality in Sri Lanka," *Scientific Reports,* no. 8 (April 1980), p. 16.

TABLE 5.5 Crude Death Rates and Infant Mortality Rates by Ethnic Group, 1962–1964

Ethnic Group	*Crude Death Rates*	*Rate Standardized for Age*	*Infant Mortality*
All races	8.6	8.6	55.1
Sinhalese	7.9	7.8	49.2
Sri Lankan Tamils	10.0	9.8	52.0
Indian Tamils	11.4	14.2	102.3
Sri Lankan Moors	10.2	10.8	62.2
Indian Moors	3.1	3.2	35.1
Burghers	9.3	6.6	33.8
Malays	7.3	5.8	47.4

Source: Sri Lanka (Ceylon), Registrar-General's Reports on Vital Statistics, 1962–1964.

TABLE 5.6 Educational Level in Estate Sector, by Sex, 1969

Educational Level	*Male*	*Female*
No schooling	26.8	56.8
Primary schooling	59.5	42.0
Middle schooling	11.7	5.6
Passed GCE O/L	1.9	0.6
Passed GCE A/L and over		0.10

Source: Socio-economic Survey, 1969.

Code of Law as the customary law of the Jaffna region and the Islamic Law as the personal law of the Muslims. This complex law system proved to be a major area of colonial intervention. The British colonial administration collected all the customary laws under the amalgam of Roman-Dutch Law and English Law, which formed the basis for the general law of the country (Jayaweera, 1984). Thereafter, traditional Sinhalese and Tamil law as well as Muslim law turned into personal laws confined by regional and religious limits and operating largely within the area of family relations.

Traditional Ceylon consisted of fairly self-contained, caste-based feudal villages and a few cities; Sinhala and Tamil communities had a rather similar life style and codes of behaviour. Only in times of political conflict did the ethnic identity seem to become a divisive factor (Jayaweera, 1984). The customary laws of both communities reflected a patriarchal social structure in which the family, with a male head of household, constituted the basic unit. The father was considered the "natural guardian" with superior family and parental authority. The wife was conceptually "dependent," confined to functions in the home (Goonesekere, 1985).

Traditional Sinhalese law was somewhat more differentiated as to the woman's position in the family. It provided women with an independent identity through property and contractual rights and a relatively liberal institution of marriage. In practice, though, the Buddhist/Sinhalese community was influenced by the contemporary status of women, conceived primarily in terms of marriage and motherhood (see Fladby, 1983).

Hindu religious tradition was formally more restrictive in sanctions on Tamil women. Women were excluded from religious rituals on grounds of "impurity and pollution." At every stage of the life cycle women were considered dependent vis-à-vis father, husband and even son.

Muslims (Malays and Moors), who arrived in Sri Lanka later in history, practiced Islamic religious law. Although purdah was not practiced thoroughly in Sri Lanka, this religious law was (and is) considered stricter than all the others as to the subordination of women. Muslim women inherit only half the share received by males. Their consent is not required for marriage, for which there exists no minimum age. Polygamy is also permitted.

During the colonial period—from the sixteenth to the mid-twentieth century—these traditional ethnic/religious customs were influenced by Christianity and Roman-Dutch law, as well as by commercial and educational activities undertaken first by the Portuguese and Dutch colonizers and later by the British. (For further historical documentation, see, among others, De Silva, 1981.) Through British influence Victorian norms of the nineteenth century were introduced to Sri Lankan society. This ideology first got a foothold among the indigenous colonial elite. Over the years, however, it slowly filtered downward into mass culture (Jayaweera, 1984).

This Victorian ideology was codified in the General Law introduced by the British. The law reinforced the patriarchal structure of society by imposing on Sri Lankan society as a whole Western norms of the husband's marital power, the monogamous indissoluble marriage and the subordination of women in the family.

As we have seen, a whole set of different ethnic/religious demands on women have operated in Sri Lankan society. In practice over the years the different ethnic/religious communities have, by and large, ascribed to the same set of norms pertaining to women's behaviour. Prominent virtues for women were chastity, docility, passivity, obedience and subservience in a life guided by demands of the household, no matter what the particular ethnic/religious contexts.[2]

These general virtues have to varying degrees in different communities and social classes in Sri Lanka been transformed into more concrete codes of behaviour. The most interesting differences seem to be influenced by class/caste rather than ethnicity. Another interesting and class/caste related variable in this respect is place of residence—urban or rural.

Culturally Defined Constraints to Action

Among the most important culturally defined limitations to women's action are the restricted freedom of movement, both physically and socially; the extreme emphasis on motherhood as the sole approved role; the limited range of activities considered appropriate for women; and the low appreciation accorded to these activities and the female sex in general (Postel and Schrijvers, 1980). In practice these limitations have diverse implications in different social classes, and they are imposed to a varying degree according to the woman's stage in the life cycle.

Generally speaking, restrictions in physical mobility apply to all class categories. Women are not supposed to travel alone. The basic purpose of this restriction has been to control female sexuality and to protect women from situations that may induce bad reputation. It is also practically difficult to combine travelling with the other responsibilities imposed on women. The regulation is manifested the way that it is considered unsuitable for a woman to ride a bicycle, drive a tractor or an ox-wagon and for young women to stay outside after dark or to leave the village without company. All situations that imply interaction with male strangers are to be avoided. Women's participation in society is naturally restrained by these rules. Concretely it means that women are traditionally prevented from participating in certain types of production (cattle rearing; to a certain extent, slash-and-burn cultivation [*shena*]; wage labour outside their home area); and women do not usually attend to the external relations of the household (market relations, political relations, or trading) (Fladby, 1983).

However, a woman's position in society and consequently the restrictions placed upon her change significantly over the life cycle. There are few differences as to the treatment of very young girls and boys. Later on distinctions become sharper, and by the age of five to ten years the separate pattern of socialization is quite manifest. During puberty the differences become even clearer: Young girls are placed completely under the authority of their parents, and restrictions pertaining to physical mobility come into force.

> Before and during her "coming-of-age" ceremony, when her first menstruation is highlighted, she is taught that from now on maintaining her good name, and subsequently procuring chances for a fortunate future, will depend on how she behaves in relationship to men. During the period of seclusion no males are allowed to enter the corner or room where the girl is kept. It is stressed that she must remain aloof of all casual, and certainly intimate connections with the other sex. She is kept indoors after dark, and told that during daytime she should avoid un-

> chaperoned contacts with the young men of the village. She is taught that a respectable girl avoids such situations and others which could arouse gossip affecting her reputation (Postel and Schrijvers, 1980:57).

An adult woman's dignity is related to her conjugal status. To remain unmarried is considered a tragedy, and widows and divorced women have lower status than women with husbands. After the birth of her first child, the status of the woman rises, and she gets her own sphere of responsibility. Gradually the woman's authority within the household is developed and restrictions on mobility decreased. By the time of menopause limitations have become scarce. The woman is not considered sexually attractive any more, and many of the responsibilities in the household have been taken over by daughters. Her reputation is consequently no longer at stake to the same extent (Postel and Schrijvers, 1980).

These general codes of behaviour must also, as mentioned, be qualified pertaining to social class. Swarna Jayaweera even states that class (as well as caste and age) is a more important variable than gender "in determining the degree of women's mobility and the focus of their activities" (Jayaweera, 1984:9).

The fact that marriage is such a basic institution in a woman's life could influence behaviour related to migration in various ways. On the one hand, it seems striking that the majority of the maids are married in view of the conjugal role women play in Sri Lankan society—the basic obligation a woman has for care of her family in a broad sense. On the other hand, according to the life cycle positions a married woman has more space in terms of freedom of movement than a virgin. As to those women who are not married before migrating, the contract in the Middle East can hypothetically influence their position on the marriage market in various ways. It may postpone the establishment of a marriage relation; it may enhance the chances of a marriage beyond social position, due to increased size of dowry; and the reverse, a woman's chances may be devalued for ideological and normative reasons.

Despite the control aspect in relation to the life cycle positions, it is striking in an international context that such a large group of married women go on contract labour abroad. Various aspects of the conjugal status of the migrants are discussed in Chapter 7.

Ideology and Reality

Normative behavioral expectations do not, of course, always reflect the realities of women's lives, although they contribute to the cultural conditioning in society. This study treats a phenomenon that clearly demonstrates how limitations on women's physical mobility and relations with the outer world are relative. Limitations prove to be elastic and may give way if this seems necessary. Long before the Middle East traffic started, the ideal type of dignified woman was a class-biased creation in Sri Lanka (as in other parts of the world). Economic imperatives have long forced nonaffluent women to work side by side with men in the fields or as labourers and consequently made these cultural codes irrelevant or unattainable. Only affluent women (of all ethnic groups) were not compelled to engage in economic activities and thus had at least the preconditions present for living by the rules. These women were restricted to their homes and dependent on their men, who mediated between them and the outside society (Jayaweera, 1984).

The economic contribution of the majority of Sri Lankan women may, however, have increased their influence in decisionmaking in the household. No comprehensive study has been undertaken concerning decisionmaking processes in Sri Lankan households, but there are indications that the picture is more nuanced and complex than traditional role expectations imply. Several studies indicate that women wield considerable power in family decisionmaking concerning housekeeping, children and questions related to household budget (Fladby, 1983b). This power is, however, often said to be "indirect and in large measure exercised behind the scenes" (Dias, 1985:147). It also varies according to ethnic community: Sinhalese women still seem to be in the strongest position to exercise decisionmaking power and Muslim women in the weakest.

Women and Extradomestic Work Prior to 1977

The national economy of Sri Lanka has long relied heavily on female labour, not only in agriculture[3] and in the informal sector but also as a stable component of the formal labour force. The use of women as a steady pool of wage labour was introduced to the island through British colonialism in the nineteenth century. Initiating a comprehensive plantation economy required large stocks of labour, in which women became the majority, particularly in the tea industry, where women were used as pickers. The great majority of these hundreds of thousands of women were imported from southern India and came to comprise an isolated part of society in the central highlands of the country. Women have consequently made up the backbone of Sri Lanka's most important foreign income earner for years.

During the colonial period, when the villages were gradually incorporated into the wider economic community, Sri Lankan women from the peasant sector also responded to market demands. The development of communication networks facilitated this process. The most common kind of employment for these women was in the urban mills, as domestic servants or in various activities in the informal sector (Jayaweera, 1984).

After independence women continued to be a source of labour in agriculture, in the informal sector, in industry (textile and food manufacturing) and in the plantation sector. The female labour force increased by 119% from 1946 to 1981, compared to an increase of 84% in the male labour force (Jayawardene and Jayaweera, 1985:131). It has been estimated that from 1946 to 1971 the proportion of females in the total economically active population increased from 22% to 26% (Postel and Schrijvers, 1980:18).[4] A labour force survey carried out by the Central Bank in 1973 (the only national study in Sri Lanka to include "housewives" as a category) reported that the percentage of women in the labour force was 45% (Central Bank of Ceylon, 1973).

A central feature of female work force participation in Sri Lanka seems, however, to be that the women systematically are concentrated in the lower levels of the employment pyramid, both in the formal and the informal sectors. The maids in the Middle East constitute a somewhat ambiguous category in this respect, being placed in the lower levels of the pyramid in some ways and at the same time having a relatively high salary.

These data on female participation in the national work force show that women's involvement in both the modern and the traditional sectors of Sri Lankan society has a long history. The data also show that women constituted a significant proportion of the total work force even before 1977. Consequently there is a gap between the ideology of the woman as a person confined to the home sphere and the reality of women out working.

Women in the Work Force After 1977

As shown in Chapter 3, the change in government in 1977 represented a significant shift in many respects. In the economic sphere several factors were mentioned, as a consequence of the adoption of the strategy of the Open Economy: import liberalization, initiation of the Free Trade Zone (FTZ) and the subsequent encouragement of foreign investment, privatization of many state sector services, devaluation. A main feature of the new economic policy has been the even stronger absorption of female labour power into economic activities at the same time as the occupational profile of this labour has undergone significant changes.

The previous government (1970–77) had in various ways tried to stimulate female employment in the handlooms sector and in handicrafts, pottery and other traditional crafts. In the 1960s female employment had increased substantially in the textile and garment sector. Policy changes associated with the Open Economy, or export-oriented industrialization, however, have meant that some of the traditional female occupations have been destabilized. This effect is particularly so with the handloom sector, where most of the over 40,000 women working there lost their jobs after 1977 (Rupesinghe, 1990).

New arenas for employment have opened up for Sri Lankan women, however, the three most significant being the Free Trade Zone, the tourist sector and the Middle East. The most important of these three, in terms of numbers employed and currency earnings for the state, is the Middle East traffic. In the FTZ 79%, or about 30,000, of the employees are women (Jayawardene and Jayaweera, 1985). In the early 1980s the tourist sector has lost some importance as a market for employment following the severe escalation of the ethnic conflict in the country.

According to statistics (see Table 5.7) the gross unemployment rate has decreased for women during the 1970s. This decrease is most clearly so for urban women, the rate dropping from 38% in 1978/79 to 25% in 1981/82.

Economy and Ideology

In Chapter 3 I examined the structural and economic background for increased female employment in general and the employment of female migrants in particular after the 1977 shift in government. My main hypothesis as to the basic cause of the Middle East exodus was that worsening economic conditions for specific strata of the population made it necessary for households to seek access to new sources of income. Multiple employment strategies were, out of necessity, applied to a greater extent. In view of the social profile of the female migrants, the phenomenon is often portrayed as a survival strategy. Although, as we will see in Chapter 8, there is much to be said for this theory, there are also certain interesting ambiguities pertaining to the socioeconomic development in the post-1977 era in Sri Lanka.[5]

In a process of modernization or commoditization where consumer goods become increasingly available in society, certain changes tend to take place simultaneously in people's expectations. In Sri Lanka the period prior to 1977 was characterized by scarcities of all kinds, a fact that partially promoted the landslide victory of the economically liberal UNP in the 1977 elections (see Chapter 3). The UNP had actively encouraged the ideology of consumerism,[6] promising the masses a better life in terms of access to new varieties of merchandise. The liberalization of imports of consumer durables after 1977 must be viewed in this light. K. Rupesinghe gives the following description of the new situation:

> The revolution in the production of consumer durables from cheap portable radios, colour televisions and video cassettes, to a wide range of household appliances, from sewing machines to refrigerators, meant that these were no longer the privilege of the ruling classes in Sri Lanka. Ready access to consumer durables and their associated images of modernization had a profound impact on young people, and acted as an instant critique towards

TABLE 5.7 Unemployment in Sri Lanka, by Sector and Sex

Sector	*Sex*	*1973*	*1978/79*	*1981/82*
Urban	Total	32.1	20.7	14.2
	Male	24.1	12.4	10.1
	Female	55.0	37.7	25.1
Rural	Total	24.5	14.6	12.0
	Male	18.3	8.7	7.3
	Female	42.4	26.3	25.3
Estate	Total	12.0	5.6	5.0
	Male	14.3	5.7	6.4
	Female	9.4	5.4	3.6
Total		24.0	14.7	11.7
	Male	18.9	9.2	7.8
	Female	36.3	24.9	21.3

Source: "Consumer Finances and Socio-economic Survey," 1973, 1978/79, 1981/82, Central Bank of Ceylon, Colombo.

ideologies of nationalism. There was particularly a manifest adoption of western dress, particularly jeans, trousers and mini-skirts. Before 1977 the consumer explosion which affected Sri Lanka, had never been within the reach of large sections of the Sri Lankan population. Up until 1977 a regime of scarcity had disposed of essential goods through the consumer co-operatives, and only the rich had access to these consumer durables (Rupesinghe, 1990).

The consumerist culture promoted by the open economy was naturally followed by intensive advertising in the media in which women played a central part. Almost a new ethos of the modern woman emerged: "the consumer par excellence, who is in search of a packaged psyche in the form of new life styles and new fashions" (Goonatilake, 1985:182). The paradox in the new situation is that this image of the modern woman is merged with customary norms of femininity and domesticity—constituting an amalgam of a new order:

> On the one hand we have the rising tide of consumerism and commercialism; goods and services familiar to the West are advertised among us, through the television, in the same manner as in the West thus making us a part of an international market. Women, in their roles as housewives and mothers, play a prominent part in these campaigns—from the woman who advertises her clean bathrooms on TV to the beauty queen who

> extols the merits of a particular brand of milk powder. . . . On the other hand, there are films which portray women as the equals of men, in politics, in banking, in spying, in fighting etc. (Jayawardene, 1985:176).

With the wide circulation of newspapers in Sri Lanka (a highly literate Third World country), as well as the gradually more extensive spread of radios and TV sets, this new consumerist culture has obviously had a tremendous impact on society. In economic terms, however, large sections of the population evidently were not in a position to benefit from these new policies. These people were observing an explosion in consumer goods around them without being able to afford a share of the bounty. In the national socioeconomic scene after 1977 poverty-stricken Sri Lankans have thus been teased into anticipating more goods while the means of getting them have been more and more difficult to achieve.

This "revolution in expectations" (Rupesinghe, 1990) is an important variable when it comes to understanding the employment strategies each and every household has followed since 1977. Economic conditions created a need for more than one income per household for new strata of the population. This was a necessity, yet often a necessity on a new level. This ambiguity, often present in processes of modernization, is sometimes difficult to grasp, as norms are under transformation and what is considered necessary is subject to redefinition. Nevertheless, for some sections of Sri Lankan society, the necessity of finding new sources of income has been (and is) of an absolute kind, legitimizing the term "survival strategy." For both categories—relative and absolute necessity—family members are urged to utilize new niches in the labour market to adjust to the new situation. Women represent the largest potential in this respect, because the majority of Sri Lankan females have not previously been involved in wage work from a young age and because the state has actively stimulated female wage employment, mainly in the tourist sector, within the FTZ and as maids in the Middle East.[7]

The revolution in expectations also helps us to understand migrants' behaviour in the more conspicuous parts of their spending patterns. Hardly any segments of Sri Lankan society have been unaffected by the new consumer ideology, although it may have affected towns and cities compared to the countryside to different degrees. The new penetrative commercialization is naturally more strongly exposed in the urban centres, in Colombo in particular, where the flow of imported goods is a dominating element on the street scene. The demonstration effect, then, may be stronger in an urban environment. In rural contexts, however, the demonstration effect may be more personalized than in an anonymous big-city setting.

Migration Among Muslim Women

As discussed previously in this chapter, women's status varies in different ethnic groups in Sri Lanka. Muslim women have traditionally been more isolated in their households, more strictly controlled by their male kin and subject to more discriminatory private laws than Sinhala and Tamil women. Consequently it might be expected that Muslim communities would be more reluctant to make the drastic decision for a woman to go abroad for two years. This expectation would apply both to the women themselves, who are used to a protected life in their respective communities, and to their husbands or fathers, whose pride and masculine identity are related to controlling "their" women.

One informant, who used to work for an NGO in a fishing village in Hambantota trying to activate local women into different income-generating and other activities, found it virtually impossible to get the Muslim women mobilized outside their own sheltered households. Although there can be many reasons for not succeeding in the mobilization of women in these kinds of activities (for example, negligible remuneration), it underscores the seeming paradox that it is easier to get these women to go all the way to the Gulf than to make them transcend the first barrier within their own communities. Almost all the women in question wanted to go to the Middle East when the possibility arose.

Several factors contribute to an understanding of this apparent paradox. In the first place Muslims on the east coast of Sri Lanka are generally very poor and have in recent years been confronted with a continuous shrinking of their traditional basis for living. In practice their cultural barriers have thus had to give way to economic needs and a modern society. This process has obviously been slow, with monetary values gradually becoming more predominant in the whole of Sri Lanka. It is therefore likely that a combination of strongly felt economic needs and a more open attitude to new norms and values has contributed to laying the ground for the migration in Muslim communities also. It should be noted in this context that in Sri Lankan Muslim societies the status of women is more liberal than in many Muslim societies elsewhere. Their intermingling with other ethnic groups probably provides part of the explanation for this distinction.

There may also be another factor contributing to an explanation in this context. It may be that the religious/cultural restrictions on women's work outside their men's direct control can be more easily put aside, since the women are completely out of sight and therefore cannot embarrass their men directly on a daily basis. This explanation can be so even though the violations of rules in the Middle East context may appear substantially more drastic.

The Muslim community in Sri Lanka is familiar with at least one aspect of life in the Gulf—its religion. This factor may contribute to the feeling of some security in connection with leaving for an alien country. This limited familiarity may have served as a legitimizing factor for the household, especially before information about actual conditions in the Middle East started to float back. Even though stories about various adverse conditions in the Gulf are readily available through returnees, one still hears this "security" argument repeated by Muslim heads of households.

Furthermore, as mentioned, Gulf households have come to specify a preference for Muslim women. As a result, agents have become more active in Muslim communities. In some places Muslim women are said to pay lower agent fees. Although this practice may be the case some places, the data presented in this work do not reflect such tendencies. As I have indicated, the agents may in fact make higher profits on Muslim women, since this category is in particular demand.

On a general level these factors may shed some light on the reason that Muslim women participate in the Middle East traffic. In Hambantota there was another, more individual factor contributing to the takeoff of migration to the Middle East. The

Sri Lankan ambassador to Saudi Arabia in the late 1970s and the early 1980s came from the township of Hambantota. When the demand first appeared for Sri Lankan housemaids, this ambassador and his family (who were still living in Hambantota in 1986) functioned as a liaison for the maids to Saudi Arabia. Quite a number of women from the whole district of Hambantota have over the years obtained contracts through this channel. The fact that a highly respectable local man like the ambassador was involved probably gave the activity added legitimacy and security in the eyes of the population. Fairly quickly other actual agents, or rather subagents for more central firms, entered the scene. This development made the picture more diversified, both as to country of destination and the general circumstances around the migration.

Considering the distinctly different religious affiliation in the two communities, the differences between the Hambantota and Colombo samples concerning norms in relation to female migration seem surprisingly small. This finding applies both to propensity to go and to behaviour in relation to the whole process. Even though there are differences in nuance as to the authority structure of the household, in practice the behaviour of the women seems to be fairly similar. Concerning number of contracts in the Gulf, though, there was significant variation between the areas, as Table 5.8 reveals.

As we can see, the propensity to go more than once is higher in Hambantota. This propensity can be explained by many factors. One possibility is that more women in Hambantota have no children or have fewer children. In addition, the stronger kin relations among Muslims may make it easier for migrants to get female relatives to take care of the children.

Initial Resources

We have seen how Sri Lankan society has undergone major economic changes since 1972, which in turn has led to transformations in other spheres of society. The consumer ideology has had an impact all the way down to the poorest sections of the population, leaving the poor with higher expectations but with limited possibilities of improving their standard of living. Money has become increasingly instrumental in achieving a

TABLE 5.8 Number of Contracts for Gulf Employment, Colombo Compared to Hambantota

Number of Contracts	*Colombo*	*Hambantota*	*% of Total*
1	66	48	63
2	28	44	31
3	6	7	6
Total %	100	99	100
N	110	27	139

respectable social status. Money has also proved the unchallenged driving force behind the Middle East migration.[8] In fact, the Marga study indicates that "the lure of money would have overridden all other considerations in accepting whatever is given" (Marga, 1986:85). The women involved take risks that they would never have taken in their own country, the majority (52%) having no specific knowledge in advance about the specific job they are undertaking for two years overseas (Marga, 1986:85). The contract consequently serves as a lottery ticket the migrant pins her hopes on because of the demonstration effect of the relative success of some neighbors.

The heavy risks taken must be explained by the very poor initial resources these people possess. Hardly any of the families have sufficient stable income to support the basic household economy. The typical migrant household keeps going through mixed employment strategies, leading a hand-to-mouth existence. The number of dependents (young children and old people) is often relatively high, leaving the families with few producers and many consumers.

Many households are also heavily in debt for various reasons common among the poor. Moneylenders have over the years established a strong grip on society, exploiting the vulnerable economic basis of the inhabitants. In addition to this already existing debt, most migrants have to borrow considerable sums to pay the agents, who often charge heavy illegal fees to establish the contract. These loans usually have to be repaid with interest of 20% per month, which obviously represents a considerable additional burden.

On top of these basic disadvantages, the female migrant households, located as they are in the lower economic end of society, usually score weakly on other social variables as well: health may be relatively poor;[9] education and language skills are limited. Deprived of basic assets like these, migrants are not likely to possess much self-esteem. Moreover, in view of the abundant supply of potential "mobile maids," the bargaining power of the individual migrant is close to nil.

Given the opportunity structure for these women in Sri Lankan society, the motivation behind the move is clearly to improve or sustain the family situation. Yet the structural conditions underlying the Middle East traffic do not provide a conducive starting point for these migrant women.

We have seen in this chapter that the women of Sri Lanka have a long history of wage labour participation. What is new after 1977 is the kind of work offered and the circumstances in which it takes place. Middle East domestic service represents a somewhat special category among the new sectors of employment for women in terms of questions of continuity and change. Housemaids working in the Gulf have an ambiguous position as to the breaking down of established norms pertaining to women and work. The kind of work undertaken fits in well with established ideology, but the action of leaving one's own family in order to work in a strange country represents a drastic break with tradition.

Class/caste and gender factors interplay in Sri Lankan society when it comes to establishing acceptable options for women at different stages in the life cycle. I have contended that class is probably the most significant parameter in this respect. The combination of class and gender points to the main background variables for explaining the composition of the work force in the Middle East. I have contended that ideological and practical barriers to leaving the confines of the family are de facto overcome for the migrants. The major hypothesis in this respect is that economy by necessity is an overriding concern for this class of people. The hypothesis does not imply that other concerns are unimportant, only that they have to involve compromises. I assume that the other concerns that may seem overruled in fact hit back, in that new sets of problems and contradictions confront the women as a result of their norm-transcending behaviour.

A related hypothesis is that women who can afford to will tend to abide by the ideology of traditional sex roles. Even though salaries in the Middle East may also seem attractive to somewhat wealthier women, the social costs are judged to be too high. If this hypothesis is so, the significance of noneconomic variables in migration decisionmaking is underlined.

Notes

1. There are, however, indications that class is more important than sex as to educational attainment. There is a generally positive attitude in Sri Lankan society toward education of girls compared with other developing countries (Jayaweera, 1985).

2. Kumari Jayawardene (1985:173) refers to this as "Brahmin ideology," even though, as she says, "the Sinhalese have no Brahmins, and the Tamil Brahmins are usually confined to ceremonial temple functions." According to this ideology, the "dos" included, among others, the virtues mentioned above. For a well-born woman, there were also several "don'ts," including "loud talk, laughing, running, idling and keeping the company of independent (therefore bad) women."

3. In this statistically invisible sector of female employment, one found (and finds) women working in paddy cultivation (weeding, transplanting, harvesting), in food processing and as independent workers in slash-and-burn cultivation. In addition, they are involved in "cottage" industries to meet consumption as well as market needs (Jayawardene and Jayaweera, 1985).

4. These figures are obviously too low. A high proportion of women's work is carried out in sectors that do not fall under the official definition of labour. The participation of women in agricultural production, e.g., is often considered an extension of their domestic roles and is thus ignored in statistics.

5. The notion of survival strategy tends to be used in a culture-relative way, and not as a question of avoiding starvation, literally speaking. However, it may occasionally in fact mean that sheer survival is at stake.

6. K. Rupesinghe (1990) defines consumerism as "the easy access to consumer durables to the masses" and sees it as a central, ideological part of export-oriented industrialization in the Third World. The ideology is labelled the "new populism" of regimes upholding this development strategy.

7. Employment is naturally a central issue for governments trying to pursue a liberal economic strategy. A "revolution in expectations" not fulfilled, at least to some minimum extent, will easily create serious frustrations, which in turn may lead to an unstable political situation.

8. There are, however, examples of women who leave for other reasons: to escape the authority of father or husband or to avoid marriage arrangements made by parents (Mook, 1991).

9. As previously stated, the migrants must undergo a health check before being accepted. These required health certificates are, however, fairly easily manipulated through bribery. (This information was often given openly from the migrant families.)

6

Status of Sri Lankan Women in the Gulf

In this chapter I will deal with the situation that confronts Sri Lankan women when they enter for their first time in their lives a completely different environment for a lengthy period of time.

In Chapter 2 we saw that domestic servants are exempted from local labour codes, leaving them nearly unprotected by law. This implies that housemaids are almost completely dependent on the goodwill of their employers when it comes to their general life situations in the Gulf. Consequently there is individual variation on this issue. Nevertheless, we can identify fairly systematic patterns, even across the different receiver countries, as to how the maids are treated. This information has been obtained through interviews with returned maids, as well as through the limited secondary material available.[1]

The clear majority of the sample in this study go to Kuwait, as Table 6.1 shows.

Expectations from the Employer and Agent

As mentioned in Chapter 2, housemaids are imported not only among rich Arab households. Because of the general increase in standard of living in the Gulf, even middle-class families can afford a housemaid from abroad. A maid from Sri Lanka is at the moment the cheapest, but she still costs a fair amount of money—salary, food and lodging, possible medical expenses and travel costs, as well as various fees to agents and the like. Consequently as much work as possible is expected from the maid while she is there. Arab households have made an investment from which they require maximum output.

TABLE 6.1 Country of Destination of Female Migrants

Country	*N%*	%
Dubai	18	13
Abu Dhabi	7	10
Kuwait	70	50
Bahrain	8	6
Saudi Arabia	11	8
Other	23	16
	140	100

Within the fairly authoritarian culture of these countries it is not surprising that employers will keep as much control over their employee as possible. The situation is probably further underscored by the discriminatory attitudes, described in Chapter 2, towards servants generally and specifically towards Third World women in such positions. The maids carry a triply low status as ethnic aliens, unskilled workers and women, rendering their position that of virtual social nonpersons (Longva, 1990).

It is in this context that we must view the often quite oppressive circumstances under which the Sri Lankan maids live and work. Generally the women are obliged to cede their passport to the employer (with the ultimate control this action involves); they are not allowed to change employment without the consent of the sponsor and/or the authorities; and they are subject to forced repatriation in cases of losing their jobs or in case they are accused of poor work performance (Spaan, 1989). Given the difference in power between the parties, it is very likely that the employer's word will count in case of a conflict; this also invariably seems to be the case, according to various sources.

Because of the probationary period described in Chapter 2, agents also continue to play a role for three months after a housemaid's arrival in the Gulf. There are cases in which the maid is forcibly held back until the probationary period is over in order to relieve the agent from his economic responsibility.

The Work Itself

The work assigned to housemaids in the Gulf ranges from cooking, serving meals, sewing and cleaning and washing (cars, clothes and carpets) to childcare and care of aged and disabled members of the household. Some maids even have responsibility for animals. The amount of work each housemaid is burdened with will necessarily depend on the size of household and how many people participate in housekeeping and childcare. It also varies according to the individual requirements of the employer. In richer houses there is often more than one servant, which means that the burden may be lighter and the chores more specialised. In the majority of the cases in the middle-class homes, however, there is only one maid, who then has to perform all tasks, sometimes even working for two households at a time.

Arab households often are very large, both in a spatial sense and in number of members (Arabs often have joint family systems, and fertility rates are high), making the job strenuous, indeed. The Colombo-Leiden survey reveals that about 45% of the domestic servants had to cover an area of between 9 and 20 rooms. The large majority (66%) had to serve, cook and clean for households of between 5 and 20 members (25% containing between 9 and 20) (Spaan, 1992). Furthermore, the very hot and dusty climate adds extra strain, as do language problems and general difficulties in communicating from such different backgrounds. The fact that housemaids live in with the employer also makes them very vulnerable as to hours on call.

The data on working conditions and living situation in this study reveal a gloomy picture. A large majority of the maids have no regulated work hours, so they are on call day and night. (See Table 6.2.)

As many as 49% of the respondents say they have a work day of more than 16 hours. Only 11% report having less than a 12-hour work day. The pattern is clearly that the women must be on call all day. Usually they are also actually working more or less all the time, being free only the few hours they may sleep.

Consequently it is no surprise that 47% report the work load to be "very hard." (See Table 6.3.) This again is a relative statement, but by breaking it down into more concrete questions, the figure seems too low rather than too high: 72% of the housemaids did not get any days off during the whole contract period, 15% got a day off once in a while, and 13% got some time off regularly (usually a few hours during the

TABLE 6.2 Work Hours for Maids in the Gulf

Work Hours	*N*	%
<12	15	11
12–16	56	41
16+	67	49
	138	101
		2 NI

TABLE 6.3 Work Load Appraised by Migrant Herself

Work Load	*N*	%
Very hard	65	47
Medium	50	36
Easy	23	17
	138	100
		2 NI

weekend to go to the mosque or the church or temple if there was one nearby).

Religious Conditions

The religion of the indigenous population in the whole Gulf area is almost exclusively Islam (Sunni, Shi'ite or Wahhabi).[2] Consequently there should be sufficient possibilities for Muslim migrants to perform their religious rituals, provided they are permitted to do so by their employers. It is not likely that the employers will hinder the maids from undertaking their daily prayers. As we will see, some maids are even taken to Mecca during their stay—usually to take care of the children of the household. Thus from a religious point of view Muslim migrants can be fairly fortunate.

For Christians the situation varies more. In some places Christian institutions are allowed to function, as in Kuwait, where the Christian church is a well-known meeting place for foreign workers. Consequently the facilities may be there to practice one's religion, but the individual maid may not be allowed out to use them.

Worst off in this connection are the Buddhist and Hindu Sri Lankans. There are only two Hindu temples in the Gulf, one in Bahrain and one in Oman. For Buddhists and Hindus the only realistic possibility is to perform religious rituals in private, unless this offends the employer—which often seems to be the case. About 50% of the Colombo-Leiden sample were forbidden to perform rituals connected to Buddhism.

Following from this it seems that for the majority of the Sri Lankan maids at present, it is difficult to lead the kind of religious life they are obliged to according to their own beliefs and customs. This may put an extra psychological burden on the women, in terms of loneliness and possibly guilt feelings.

Savings

As has been indicated, the Sri Lankan housemaids live under extremely controlled and isolated conditions while in the Gulf. They are usually kept on call within the house, let out only if accompanied by "madam." Ironically these conditions have certain favorable aspects when it comes to possibilities for saving money. Compared to male expatriates, who at least have freedom of movement (sometimes also within limits) and some spare time outside the work site, the domestic lives of housemaids provide few possibilities for squandering their salaries. They are provided with food, lodging and sometimes also clothing and medical care if necessary. (The quality of these goods may vary significantly, however.) Air fare home is also supposed to be paid by the employer.[3] Thus the housemaids as a category seem to constitute the professional group in the Gulf with the highest rate of saving. However, the net financial outcome of the stay is much lower than for most male migrants, as maids' salaries are far below the male standard.

Accommodations and Social Life

Depending on the kind of household the maid is working for, she will often be in fairly luxurious material surroundings. She herself may even benefit from some of the luxury by having access to tap water, a water toilet, electric fans, a TV set and radio. The houses are often constructed in an isolating manner, however, with high walls and small windows that make it difficult to contact people outside the premises. Besides, Arab-Islamic codes of behaviour restrict the possibilities for domestic servants to go outside the home without being accompanied by the employer. The degree to which this is actually complied with may vary, individually and by country. But various sources suggest that the freedom of movement among Sri Lankan maids is very limited. For the majority of the maids the only opportunities to go out are the occasional visits or outings of the family, in which case the maids are brought along to serve meals and look after children. Quite a number of the maids are also taken along with "madam" to shop. Usually they are then obliged to wear an overgarment together with a veil, making them unrecognizable to others. The most frequent way of keeping contact with the outside world for the housemaids is actually by telephone (if allowed), writing letters and sending cassettes.

As Table 6.4 shows, 32% of the women interviewed for this study were not allowed out of the house at all, and 47% could leave with the employer whenever he or she decided to go out (usually to go shopping or to accompany the family on outings and trips to take care of the children). In addition, 21% could go out alone when they were allowed to (usually during work hours to shop or do other errands for the wife).

Concerning freedom to meet other Sri Lankan housemaids in the same area, 37% of the returnees interviewed reported never having been allowed to do so, 41% met other housemaids once in a while under the employer's supervision, and 23% could meet friends alone if they had any spare time. There are however, ways of circumventing such rules, which are spelled out later in this chapter. The overall picture is nevertheless one of isolation, extremely hard work and few openings for recreation and rest.[4]

The figures presented in the tables are by and large backed up by the Marga investigation. According to the Marga figures, 57% of the migrants were denied any form of entertainment, 27% could participate in religious activities (mostly Muslim), 5% could meet other Sri Lankans, and 0.9% said they had social contact with locals.

Authority Structure and Maltreatment

Sri Lankan women, coming from traditionally male-dominated societies, probably find an even more oppressive system

TABLE 6.4 Freedom of Movement for the Housemaid

Outside Household	*N*	%
Allowed alone	29	21
With employer	65	47
Not allowed	44	32
		100
		2 NI

in this respect in the Gulf. The gender situation is further reinforced by their social position as servants. The man in the house has undisputed authority, even though the maids often experience "madam" as the "evil in the system," as she is the closest in line. Physical and psychological maltreatment seem not infrequent, most often executed by the chief woman of the house. Sometimes children are allowed to carry on with harassment of various kinds.

Sexual abuse by the man of the house apparently does take place from time to time, although this naturally is hard to detect for reasons of shame and loss of reputation of the woman. When such cases are discovered (for example, when the maid gets pregnant), the housemaid is almost always the one to be blamed—often being accused of having had a relationship with some strange man from outside the house. Pregnancy seems to imply automatic repatriation.

The sexual abuse underscores a striking cultural intragender confrontation in the situation, where gender and sexuality intervene in the ethnic/class hierarchy in the household. The maids have been described as virtual social nonpersons in the Arabian home. Yet at the same time, through their womanhood, they are conceived of as potential threats by the lady in the house. Within Islamic culture female sexuality, particularly when uncontrolled by marriage, acts as a perturbing factor for men, especially so when it is introduced from outside the kinship boundaries into their private setting, where male-female interaction is frequent and open. When the men in the household abuse the maid sexually, they make her violate the Islamic code for sexual behaviour and also leave her in an extremely delicate situation in relation to the Arab women in the house. This setting nevertheless reveals an ambiguity of the housemaid's position at her workplace (Longva, 1990).

Generally speaking, this is a shady area of investigation, one in which data are extremely difficult to control. There can be various reasons for the women to want either to hide or to overcommunicate the bad conditions experienced in the Gulf, depending on the kind of grievances they have suffered. Sexual abuse committed by the employer is of course a particularly sensitive area; the abused woman would probably try to hide as much as possible, owing to shame and humiliation. One way of finding out about these matters is to ask each returned migrant whether she knows of anyone who suffered from this abuse. Through this method (which also has its weaknesses) many stories were disclosed. Even though it is impossible to treat this phenomenon in terms of numbers, an estimation made by a Sri Lankan social worker engaged in the migration traffic indicates that approximately 7% of the maids have been insulted sexually while in the Gulf. Another early study undertaken by the Women's Bureau in Colombo (1981) indicates similar findings (8 out of a sample of 100).

One indicator of the hardship the women must endure overseas is the question of premature return home. Of the total number of migrants in this study 38% had broken the contract once, and 4% had broken 2 or more contracts. Table 6.5, based on the Colombo and Hambantota interviews nevertheless shows that only a very low percentage (5%) of the respondents give maltreatment as the reason for breaking the Gulf contract and returning home prematurely.

We see that the reason most often cited for breaking the contract is illness (either of workers themselves or family members at home) or death of relatives. The real distribution in this respect may be different, as the maids may fabricate reasons for their premature return. They may state, for example, "too hard work" when the actual cause was sexual abuse. The core of the matter, nevertheless, is that the working conditions were somehow unbearable.

Other studies show similar results in this respect, although the reasons for returning early may have a somewhat different distribution. (See Korale et al., 1985:70; Eelens and Schampers, 1986.)

Escape Routes

Having underlined the weak resource base of the mobile maids from Sri Lanka, we should note the striking creativity

TABLE 6.5 Reasons for Female Migrants Breaking the Gulf Contract

Reason	*N*	%
No break	80	58
Illness/death in family	30	22
Too hard	12	9
Maltreated	7	5
Other	9	7
	138	101
		2 NI

the women demonstrate when it comes to circumventing difficulties overseas. Stories the women tell from their work reflect how they have manipulated employer control in a variety of ways. Maids not allowed out of the house use the telephone extensively when not observed by "madam"; they may arrange meetings with other maids working close by when "taking out the garbage"; they may lie and say they are Catholics in order to be let out on Sundays to attend Mass, in reality meeting other fake Sri Lankan "Catholics"; and not least, they send a letter home, asking for a telegram saying "Hurry home, mother is very sick," or other words to that effect. This last example is often heard of, even though it is a quite desperate and irreversible move.[5] The existence of this last strategy has made some employers forbid the maids to have any contact with their families in Sri Lanka. The ways the maids get around this restriction are also various. Some, whenever they get a chance, give letters or cassettes to other Sri Lankan housemaids nearby or to street cleaners working in the area. Some even tell stories of leaving their letters with a note for the garbage collector in the garbage can to avoid detection by their employers (Spaan, 1992). These stories could be supplemented further. The point is that the migrants inventively create their own escape routes within the given rough circumstances in order to survive mentally.

The Process Conditions

Once the Sri Lankan woman finds herself in an Arab household somewhere in the Gulf, various conditions influence the possibility of a successful stay. Grim stories are abundant. Some women are swindled by the recruitment agencies (apart from the illegal fees charged) and find upon arrival that no job has been arranged. Quite a number of the migrants report that they do not get their salaries in accordance with the contract. Often salary is held back as a punishment if the maid does not satisfy the employer in one way or the other. Some of the women cannot cope with the considerable physical and mental pressure often involved in the jobs. As we have seen, the working conditions are in most cases physically hard and mentally strenuous. Other women may be called home because of illness or other problems in the family. Finally, the women may simply be confronted with bad luck of various kinds.

It seems that the mobile maids are strikingly susceptible to calamities of various kinds. This observation should probably not be surprising considering their low score on initial resources, that is, their low class position. Deprived of important basic resources, the housemaids easily become objects of exploitation. Likewise, bad conditions at home—social and healthwise—may frequently cause illness and other problems and make it impossible for the maid to complete the contract. We thus see that at the outset the class position of the maids most probably influences the quality of the stay. Their lack of self-esteem may make them relatively more servile, which may influence the attitude of the employer negatively.

By contrast, the process conditions for these women could therefore be worse than for better-off women, who would possibly have approached the situation with more dignity, consequently calling forth other responses from the employer. Their home situation would probably also be more conducive to a favorable stay. These considerations are quite hypothetical, though, since hardly any resourceful middle-class women go.

There are certain striking paradoxes present in this realm. We have seen that a large number of the female migrants are faced with a truly burdensome situation overseas. This circumstance adds to the homesickness and probably to their appreciation of their own family relations in Sri Lanka while they are away. At the same time they are exposed to another world in a double sense: They experience a culture that is thoroughly alien to them, and they get insight into the fairly luxurious life middle- and upper-class Arabs lead in the Middle East. The material contrast to their own communities in Sri Lanka must be overwhelming. This contrast factor most likely contributes to maintaining the pull force when maids return with pictures from their premises abroad. The standard of living they are exposed to in the Gulf may to a certain degree even influence their own spending priorities upon their return.

However, the central process conditions are only necessary, not sufficient, preconditions for a successful end result. An important aspect—or stage—of the whole migration course takes place outside the Gulf, and in part, after the work is completed.

Notes

1. Very little research has been undertaken within the Gulf area itself because of the delicacy of the issue and the practical field problems that follow from this fact. On the national level the countries regard foreign labour as a sensitive question with no short-term solution (see Chapter 2). On the household level the sensitivity of the issue will most likely depend on the way the family in question treats servants.

2. This section is based almost entirely on material from the Colombo-Leiden investigation, particularly Spaan (1992).

3. There are, however, a number of examples in which the employer has tried to avoid this obligation by firing the employee prior to the expiration of the contract in order to place this burden on the migrant (Spaan, 1992).

4. Working conditions vary, however, from country to country in the Gulf. Restrictions seem to be most severe in Saudi Arabia in every respect, whereas Kuwait and Bahrain score most favorably.

5. This manipulated return underscores the uncertainties of the figures on reasons for premature return home.

7

Local Level: Communities, Households and Individuals

As was discussed in the theoretical section, the macro-setting impinges on the individuals in terms of facilitators and barriers when it comes to migration decisionmaking. These facilitators and barriers are variable forces according to community characteristics, household conditions and individual dispositions.

I have so far concluded that the overriding motivation of the migrants is to improve or maintain the quality of life for the whole family. Visible signs of this motivation should be observable in the local communities and households from which the migrants come. According to the progress rationale we would expect to see improvements in living conditions in terms of housing, clothing and possibly economic activities in the migrant households.

The facilitators and barriers listed in the theoretical section interplay locally and determine for the individuals and the households whether the original intentions are fulfilled or not. Cumulative processes may play an important part in the explanations for desirable or undesirable results of the chain of actions. These microprocesses become particularly important when the performance of the migrants is not as expected according to the basic rationale.

In the following section the microlevel will be handled through a presentation of the data that were collected in two local communities—Colombo and Hambantota—in Sri Lanka.

Colombo

Shanty Canal: A Description

The area has existed as a shantytown for about thirty years. The "town" is located along a water canal that runs east-west in the southern part of Colombo. There are houses on both sides of this canal close to the water. Since the late 1970s the area has expanded a great deal, so that houses have been established also in rows farther away from the canal. Originally the land was occupied illegally by the settlers, who put up shacks from whatever material they could find. The state still owns the land, but no one has tried to clear the area, and some facilities like tap water and electricity are provided to a certain extent. There are approximately 3,000 households altogether in the Shanty Canal area, the great majority being Sinhala and Buddhist.

The area is considered rough in the sense that there are heroin problems, fairly widespread prostitution and a high criminality rate. The shanty is not a very healthy place to live, being located so close to the dirty canal water. Most dwellers express a wish to move somewhere else if at all possible.

Some social programmes have been introduced in the area through various foreign and international NGOs undertaking humanitarian work of different kinds. A programme to train social workers recruited from the shanty itself has seen some progress, and quite a number of these workers function as resource persons in the area, initiating activities for women and children as well as giving advice on various matters. Through these programmes, the whole shanty has been studied thoroughly, so that information on various dimensions is available. These local social workers were important sources of information in the context of this study.

Generally speaking, it was fairly easy to get respondents to talk openly about Middle East matters. Living at such close quarters, most shanty dwellers are used to little privacy. People know a lot about each other, and they are quick to tell stories about their neighbors, which made it possible to check information from different angles. As is the case in many poor slum pockets, family life is often quite disorderly, in that infidelity is fairly common, as are divorces (mostly informal). Drinking and gambling are widespread among the men in the area and are referred to by the women as a considerable social problem.

The rate of unemployment is very high, and most households sustain themselves on multiple employment strategies; several household members (including the older children) may contribute some income, however little. Income-generating activities are varied, primarily within the field of buying and selling or home production of foodstuffs. Smaller children often contribute through begging, so the school drop-out rate is high. Income-generating activity within each household can be fairly low, however. Many men can be seen around the houses in the middle of the day, doing nothing but socializing with the other men. Their sole option is often to create some economic space for themselves within the crowded informal sector, an option that many men view as not worth the effort.

Since the late 1970s the possibility of going to the Middle East has provided some economic breathing space in the shanty. In the densely populated slum areas of Colombo, the phenomenon spread quickly with the help of active recruiting agents who promised salaries that far exceeded the level any of the household members could possibly achieve in Sri Lanka. Once this traffic started in an area a vast number of women left for the Gulf after a fairly short while. The demonstration effect has been strong, indeed.

In 1986 anyone walking around in the Shanty Canal area could fairly easily locate the houses in which a member had been working in the Middle East. These houses were generally much better than the regular shanty houses. Usually they were made of brick or wood, with wood or metal sheets on the roof. The quality of the construction could vary, but generally these new houses kept the rain out and sometimes provided an extra room for the family. The regular Shanty houses were made of different sorts of material, whatever was available when the house was raised—wood sheets, cadjan, (palm leaf) mud, pieces of wood—often in a mixture.

The Middle East women themselves often bore signs of their recent jobs abroad. They had better dresses, and sometimes they wore gold jewelry. Inside the houses the signs were even more prominent. A recurrent pattern was trinkets and gadgets on display in the main room. Preferences went along the same lines, by and large, although some peculiar specialties would pop up in different pockets, illustrating the conformity pressure concerning what to get out of a Gulf contract. The specialty could be a small ceramic figure of Venus de Milo in one area, a miniature Eiffel Tower thermometer or empty bottles of fine brandy in others.

In the cases where nothing had been done to improve the housing standard, the explanation given was "nothing left of the money." The reasons could be many: The family had to use all the money on daily subsistence, as it was a big household without any income worth mentioning; the family had been swindled by the agent or the employer; or the receiver of the money back home had squandered most of it. Often households had been heavily in debt before the contract, so that much of the salary had to go into interest payments before any savings could be made.

It was interesting to see that so many of these households gave high priority to improving their housing in the Shanty Canal area, even though most of them stated that they would like to escape the area if at all possible. Most people had probably realized that the foreign income would not suffice to move out and settle somewhere else anyhow, so they might as well make the best of the situation where they were. Still, people with improved houses mentioned that if and when they were going again, they would give high priority to buying land and setting up a new home outside the Shanty.

In this context there may be a bias in the sample. The people interviewed within the shanty may have been the unsuccessful ones who did not manage to move and resettle. According to the informants from the area, however, very few people had actually moved out of Shanty Canal at all. The few who had moved had joined relatives with property somewhere else. An important exception in this respect were the young girls who used the foreign job partly to amass dowry and subsequently managed to climb socially through marriage. This proportion is, however, likely to be fairly small; the majority of the women were already married (60%), and a majority of the unmarried migrants reported that very little had been saved for their future. The young unmarried girls are usually sent as an asset for the household, which most likely does not have any viable income and which expects loyal support from the daughter. Some young girls, however, had apparently managed to marry into a better life outside the slum.

Since labour migration started from the area, the costs of establishing a contract have risen gradually. Agent fees have risen steadily over the years, and the general inflation has also hit all the other expenses attached to the traffic. However, since this migration has been established for some time in various areas of Colombo, the network advantage has become more prominent. It has become easier to get a contract without going through an agent than it used to be. Workers may have established a new contract themselves in the Gulf before leaving or may have received tickets through relatives or friends working abroad. Even though such favours done by friends and even relatives more frequently have to be paid for, this procedure is much cheaper than going through an agent. Nevertheless, 60% of the sample got their contracts through a recruiting agent; 38% of the sample had borrowed money privately at a rate of 20% per month, and 55% at a rate of 15–20% per month, to pay the various expenses related to establishing a contract. This heavy initial debt burden obviously reduces the value of a contract, depending on how much they have to borrow. Often the migrant has to work for a long period in the Gulf to repay debts related to the establishment of the contract, as well as other previous debts.

This general indebtedness often put extra pressure on the women to go for more than one contract. Women who could somehow get a stand-in to take care of the house and the children almost invariably said they wanted to go back for another contract—even if they had had a traumatic experience last time they went. Of the Colombo sample 66% had been to the Gulf only once, and about 90% of these returnees said they wanted to go again if possible, 28% had been there twice, and 6% three times.

The general picture of the Colombo sample is that very few households manage to pull themselves out of the vicious circles of poverty through the Middle East labour migration. The quantitative illustration of different facets of this observation is presented later in this chapter. In the following sections two streets in the northern part of Colombo will be handled as a separate case study, as they represent a somewhat different scene within the same general frame of reference.

Alutmahawatha/Vestwyke Avenue

These two streets are located not far from the harbour, in a former poor housing area with a fairly mixed ethnic composition. The two communities are known to be quite violent, with a serious and growing heroin problem and a general high rate of criminality. Abuse of alcohol and family breakups were also reported to be fairly widespread. The population used to live under very poor housing conditions and had a high rate of unemployment or underemployment. Quite a number of the men in the area used to work on and off at the harbour; some were petty traders or into the unspecified field of "various odd jobs."

In 1980 Alutmahawatha was selected by the Norwegian NGO Redd Barna (a branch of the Save the Children Foundation) as the target of a housing scheme cum community development programme. Vestwyke Avenue was selected in 1983. The approximately 120 households in the two streets were given a loan of Rs 13,000 each, together with instructions on how to open a bank account and how to deal with money in an organized manner. It was a precondition for getting the loan that a saving book had been established. The loan was earmarked for house construction, and the inhabitants got help to put up the house. One person in the household (usually the man) was given responsibility for handling the loan. The minimum rate of debt repayment was set at Rs 100 per month.

A visitor who came to these two streets in 1986 without knowing the history could easily believe that this was a fairly respectable middle-class area. Houses were generally attractively plastered, sometimes decorated with ceramic tiles and flower arrangements in front. The small walkways between the houses were nicely kept, and the whole area gave a fairly clean impression. Moreover, the houses were usually well furnished and decorated inside.

What had happened was that after this housing scheme was introduced the Middle East traffic started in the whole general area. As usual, the phenomenon spread quickly. Having begun to improve their housing in an organized manner seems to have encouraged the inhabitants to continue even further. Hardly any of the existing houses in the two streets could have been constructed on only Rs 13,000. Quite a number cost more than Rs 50,000, some possibly even more than Rs 100,000. All the money each household could pool had been directed into house building and house decoration. Apparently a combination of two factors had influenced the behaviour of the inhabitants in the area. First, the idea of having a nice home for the family had been helped into realization through the Norwegian programme. Second, the programme meant that the target families had received budget training that introduced planning of the household economy to a certain extent.

Subsequent exposure to the Middle East migration, with the possibilities of having access to relatively large remittances, stimulated the families to strive even further concerning their house-building projects. Consequently it seemed that these former slum dwellers, through some economic education and favorable circumstances, could utilize the Middle East option in a more cumulative way than in other Colombo slum areas. This tendency was so even though the employment pattern and people's general behaviour had not differed substantially from that of other slum pockets in the past; regular household economies were by and large of a casual kind, the men working on and off in various odd jobs, particularly related to the harbour. The spending pattern of the households had varied considerably, depending on whatever sources of income were there. Saving had been a rare phenomenon.

The striking standard of the housing in these two streets can be slightly misleading when discussing consequences of female Middle East migration. The very best houses is the area (two-story houses with ceramic decorations and expensive woodwork) belonged to households where the man had been to the Gulf at least once. This applied to six houses altogether. Although these houses definitely contributed to lifting the overall impression of the area, these two streets clearly have a higher general housing standard than other slum areas.

Most of the households still had at least one female member in the Middle East and intended to continue this pattern in the foreseeable future. The inhabitants could not see any other source of income in Sri Lanka that could replace the level they had reached through migrating to the Gulf. Many of the households (particularly the male members) expressed a wish to invest in "some business" once the house was completed and the loans repaid. The recurring preference in this respect was predominantly some sort of trading, for example, in fish or shrimp. Apart from whatever amount they had to set aside for daily consumption (usually at least Rs 1,500 per month in these households), a high proportion of the respondents said they intended to save money in a bank account in order to invest later on. No one had so far come to that stage, as most houses were not yet completed. Some people had obviously overstretched their capacity by aiming at a two story house from the beginning. The first contract had enabled them to complete parts of the first floor only.

With cash available another possibility was to enter the rather flourishing moneylending business. This niche had apparently been utilized by a number of people with connections to the Middle East traffic in both streets—about nine people in Alutmahawatha and five in Vestwyke. These figures are, however, quite uncertain, as this business, being illegal if not registered, belongs to the most shady area of the local economy, particularly since the moneylending business has increasingly become linked with the heroin trade. Apart from this latter field, the Middle East traffic as such provides a thriving exchange ground for moneylenders. Middle East recruiting agents in the area have become expensive in recent years; Rs 5,000–8,000 for a contract is not unusual. Not having such large amounts in ready cash, potential migrants have to borrow money to establish a foreign work contract. As the local interest rate is 20% per month, the lenders are left with a nice profit. A high proportion of the migrants (male and female) in the area had had to rely on such lenders. Tamils in the area may also have had to bribe certain officials to get a valid passport.

Generally speaking, informants living or working in the area emphasized that competition and striving for status had grown much worse in the wake of migration. The climate had hardened, and the attitude of "never trust anybody" had become more prevalent. Although these societies had also been quite competitive, the means had changed in a more material direction. Earlier, education had been a more significant vehicle for social mobility. "If you can't beat your neighbors in education, at least you can show off moneywise," one of the informants commented.

In a certain sense Middle East migration has served to reduce the importance of education. Not only is schooling deflated in terms of status, its importance as a way of climbing the social and economic ladder is also reduced. Young people see little point in investing in education when money apparently is more easily made elsewhere. Upgrading money at the expense of education in obtaining status had also led to some reshuffling of the social layers in the area. The relatively less resourceful households had a chance to compete on new terms. The real losers in the area seem to be those who do not have any possibility of sending anyone abroad. The contrast between those households and the migrant households was clearly visible. Of 67 houses in Alutmahawatha, only 5 had not been able to pay minimum interest to Redd Barna of Rs 100 a month for the original loan. None of these houses had any connections with the Middle East business. The reasons that households did not send anyone to the Middle East were the same as in most other communities. Either they did not have anyone available in the household to send, or they did not have ready arrangements for childcare and housekeeping. Except for two households everybody expressed a desire to go, if possible.

Material striving seemed to have reached an even higher stage in Vestwyke than in Alutmahawatha. In Vestwyke the migration had already started when the housing programme was introduced. This factor contributed to completing the scheme much more quickly than in Alutmahawatha. In Vestwyke people by and large gave even higher priority to conspicuous items and details.

The relatively better conditions in Alutmahawatha and Vestwyke compared to most other migrant-sending communities in Colombo can be attributed mostly to the combination of the two factors—the Norwegian scheme and the Middle East option—in which some training in economic planning is a central point. However, these factors alone cannot explain the whole scene, as the women's remittances were usually not enough to raise the standard to such an extent in a short while, even considering the economic planning and the basic loan. Consequently there must have been other assets available in addition to these sources.

If we leave aside the households in which the man had one or more contracts in the Middle East since these families obviously belong to another economic category, the men's income must still point to a central part of the explanation. Even though unemployment and underemployment are reported to be high in the area, the work that men undertake on and off, particularly in the harbour, is better paid than many of the other possibilities available to this category of unskilled labour. A high proportion of the men in the area must have continued this work, at least to a certain extent, while the women were in the Gulf, so that the foreign earnings could go into housing more or less in toto. Additionally, there were the more dubious income possibilities attached to moneylending and the heroin trade. According to local sources these shady businesses were significant elements of the local economy, especially related to the Middle East traffic. However, they are difficult to map or quantify.

The more lasting local income possibilities are central to any assessment of the prospects for these communities when and if the Middle East option dries up or the individual households do not have the possibility of sending anyone abroad for another contract. It looks as though these two streets do have better prospects in an economic sense than many other migrant pockets, due to the favorable starting conditions. The social climate is disturbing, however, as the increased circulation of money has intensified local conflicts and apparently contributed to an increase in the abuse of alcohol and drugs. Nor is the social tension likely to decrease in case of a phasing out or a cut in the Middle East traffic. Now that the inhabitants have been exposed to a new level of consumption and a generally better material standard of living, any material and social regress is going to be extremely painful.

Alutmahawatha and Vestwyke provide us with at least one positive lesson: the importance of training the potential and actual migrating population in how to deal with money when it suddenly flows in more abundantly than ever before.

Hambantota

The largest share of the Hambantota sample was picked in Muslim fishing communities in the township of Hambantota itself. Additional samples came from one nonfishing community located inland close to the town, one rural Muslim village approximately 100 kilometers northeast of Hambantota town, as well as the special case of "Gallegama" village in the western part of the district. This last case study will be handled separately later.

The communities outside the township of Hambantota were chosen primarily to check on whether there were significantly different patterns of behaviour in fishing and nonfishing Muslim communities. As a general observation we may say that the similarities are more striking than the diversities between these communities, although there are interesting differentials on a more detailed level.

In the following section the main emphasis is on findings in Hambantota town and variation between the different communities there.

Hambantota Town

The township of Hambantota is the largest densely populated area near the large eastern national park of Yale. The town is a Grama Sevaka Division with a total population of about 9,000, or roughly 1,000 households. Hambantota has a natural harbour, the name meaning "the place where Muslims anchor their boats." The town is the centre for the district administration, and administration is the most important source of income besides fishing and salt manufacture. Salt processing used to be a major enterprise in Hambantota but is in decline. Apart from being an administrative centre, Hambantota serves other functions. There are three mosques, three Buddhist temples and one church within the confines of the town. There are also four schools (one Muslim), a hospital, a police station, a post office, a telegraph agency and a petrol station. A big luxury hotel has been finished just outside the town, supplementing the existing guest houses. Hambantota, however, has never been established as a tourist resort. In the town one also finds a market, lots of small shops, tea shops and quite a number of "toddy-shops" or "tavernas," which are local bars with easy access to liquor.

There has been a considerable population increase: between 1971–81 the increase for Hambantota was 25% (340,000 to 424,000), as compared to 17% for the country as a whole. Population density has been unevenly distributed, the most populated areas being in the west where rainfall is heaviest. This distribution has meant strong pressure on land over the years, to the extent that there is now a fairly strong internal migration to the eastern divisions of the district (Census of Population and Housing, 1971 and 1981). Consequently the pressure on land has increased considerably also in the dry zone areas of the district. The economic basis for the population at large in Hambantota has shrunk significantly over the years, partly because of this population increase. There are far fewer opportunities to carry out the traditional slash-and-burn cultivation than before. Untouched jungle areas are fewer, and much of the remaining forest is being removed (York Smith, 1986).

There is a marked scarcity of paid employment opportunities in the district, as well as considerable seasonal unemployment and underemployment in agriculture and fishing. According to official statistics 19% of the economically active population is registered as unemployed, a figure that should be handled with care as defining this category is extremely uncertain in agricultural and fishing communities.

Two-thirds of the district population live below the official poverty level of Rs 300 per household per month, which entitles them to food stamps. The economic setbacks that have been strongly felt among the poorest sections of Sri Lankan society since the late 1970s have obviously hit the Hambantota population hard.

This information, however, serves only as a general background for an impression of the economic conditions and the prospects for the district at present. So far Hambantota has supplied about 2% of all Sri Lankan migrant workers (both men and women) to the Gulf, which is about average for nonurban areas outside Colombo (Korale et al., 1985). If then, Hambantota has been more badly affected by economic problems, it had not (to 1984) resulted in a more widespread migration than is the case elsewhere, although there is not necessarily a direct relationship between an economic need and the act of migration, as so many other factors are of importance (access to information, agencies, family conditions). No official figures are available as to the sex component of the contingent from Hambantota, but there are reasons to believe that the majority are women and also that the share of women is increasing. This development is occurring mainly because Muslim women are in demand, as mentioned earlier, and because the Hambantota District now has become established as a sender area, with more contacts and a facilitating network. Consequently it is not unlikely that the 2% share has increased.

In the town about one-half of the population is Muslim, distributed fairly equally between the two ethnic groups, Malay and Moor. No important differences between these two ethnic Muslim groups were uncovered for my purposes. Both groups are referred to as Muslims in this context, which is also what they call themselves when asked about which ethnic group they belong to. The Muslims are the successors of Arab traders who came to the coast many centuries back. Initially they were traders only, but for the last two centuries they have also been involved in fishing. The different ethnic communities have been used to a peaceful coexistence over the years, and intermarriage has occurred.[1]

Three communities—or actually three streets—were subject to interviewing: (1) Urban Counsel Quarters (UC Quarters), (2) May Street and (3) Mariya Road. These three areas had a high number of migrants and were predominantly Muslim. Referring to these three streets as "fishing communities" needs some qualification. It is correct to say that a great number of the inhabitants were involved in fishing in one way or another some years back, although there were always people involved in other activities, like trading and even some sort of public employment. In May Street and Mariya Road a majority of the people still consider themselves "fishermen" (only men carry out the fishing itself in this area of the country), irrespective of the actual situation. In the UC Quarters the picture is more varied. People state more firmly that "fishing is no good these days" and that there are few possibilities for fishermen anymore. Some people in that street still go out fishing once in a while, and some are occasionally involved in related activities like fish trading. All three streets had been poor communities by and large; almost all households were food stamp receivers before the Middle East traffic started.

The housing conditions constituted a fairly important difference in this context. The Urban Counsel Quarters, as the name indicates, were originally constructed about thirty years ago with official funds for the (presumably) most needy people in the area. After twenty years the rent to the state had paid for the houses. Consequently almost all the people in the UC Quarters owned their homes themselves. Although a bit worn, these houses were of a fairly good standard: two to three rooms, made of solid brick with sheet or tiled roofs. Superficially, therefore, these households appear better off than the other communities, and to a certain extent this is true. In Mariya Road there are also a few government houses (Fishing Quarters) that have been constructed more recently. The people living there are still paying a rent of Rs 50 per month, based on the same principle as in the UC Quarters.

Fishing Societies

Certain characteristics of Hambantota, particularly the fishing communities, need to be dealt with more in depth in order to understand the context behind labour migration activity. First, most of the inhabitants of the fishing communities in Hambantota were poor, and a high proportion were food stamp recipients. Certain characteristics of the fishermen's way of life make some qualification necessary. Generally speaking, the fishermen were used to living from day to day, spending money "extravagantly" after a good catch and subsequently living from whatever little there might be. The communities have been marked by absence of economic planning, so that their level of consumption has fluctuated greatly. One factor that to a certain extent has modified this picture has been a tendency to buy gold jewelry in good periods and to sell or pawn it when times changed. This activity should not be overemphasized, as buying gold necessitated above-average assets, but it is an interesting phenomenon that seems to be revitalized now in the wake of Gulf migration.

Despite being Muslim, these fishing communities have also been known as "rough" societies characterized by hard work and heavy drinking, particularly during periods of no work. Abuse of alcohol was a problem mentioned by many women in the area and also caused economic worry. A bottle of *arrac* (the local liquor) cost about Rs 50 (1986), about half the daily remittance from the Middle East. In Hambantota township prostitution was also reported to be a problem, particularly in some fishing areas. Some people seemed to believe that prostitution had become worse after the migration started and that some of the returned migrants had entered that trade. Such information is, however, difficult to ascertain.

The unstable economic basis of these societies explains why moneylenders have gained such a powerful position over the years. This observation does not, however, apply only to the fishermen's households; the whole district is marked by the control of moneylenders.

Traditional small-scale fishing has had serious problems in the area. Resource prospects are also grim, according to local experts. Consequently an increasing number of households that used to rely on fishing for their daily living have had to look for other sources of income. Lack of faith in fishing is indicated by the fact that only very few of the migrants consider investing their Gulf money in fishing. The ones that do spend money in this field usually buy an outboard motor for the traditional catamaran (*oru*), if they own one themselves, to make the task physically easier. Obviously, however, this purchase does not solve the basic problem of scarce resources.

In the following sections the situation in the township of Hambantota will be discussed in general terms, based on observation, interviews and talks with informants. Then data from the two Hambantota nonfishing villages will be drawn for comparison. Main emphasis will be placed on material aspects such as housing, consumption and capital formation.

Three Streets in Hambantota: Similarities and Differences

The UC Quarters started the Middle East traffic as early as 1979. After a few years other communities in Hambantota entered the field as well. As mentioned, similarities prevail when we compare the UC Quarters, May Street, and Mariya Road. One conspicuous difference at first glance, however, is the standard of housing. Middle East houses in the UC Quarters were generally of a much higher quality than in the other two streets. Some of the houses were close to a Colombo middle-class standard. Communication with the inhabitants revealed a quite complex picture that qualified this initial impression of a fairly well-off community. First and foremost, almost every household in the area was involved in the migration. This finding was also confirmed by data from the Planning Unit. The two nonmigrating households in the sample "did not have the possibility of going," they stated, as the woman in the one house was too old and in the other house "they did not have enough money to pay the agent."

Since people living in the UC Quarter all had fairly good houses in the first place, they did not have to make the same major investment as was the case with people who had been living in cadjan huts. What is interesting is that even though their homes were quite adequate beforehand, they gave high priority to making them even better. Fairly large sums were spent on extending and improving the UC Quarter houses, with Rs 75,000 the largest amount spent to this effect. Due to the favorable starting point the impression after a few contracts was quite striking in some cases. In this context (which resembles the Vestwyke/Alutmahawatha cases discussed previously) the visitor may easily be deceived by this conspicuous first impression—or at least deceived to a certain extent. It is true that the households have put a solid amount of capital in their houses and that this represents an investment that is fairly safe, in the sense that it is not likely to fall drastically. At the same time, however, many of these households are still very poor when it comes to assets for daily living.

A high proportion of the inhabitants either had no other source of income than the Middle East employment or the income they could earn in Hambantota was far from sufficient for subsistence. A majority had already been to the Gulf twice and would readily go again if the opportunity arose.

None of the households with a female migrant had made any investment apart from home improvements. A few households that had sent one woman twice but did not see the possibility of another contract had started selling off the goods they had brought from the Gulf. This pattern is fairly common all over and is maintained until there is nothing left to sell. None of the migrants from the UC Quarters had had to sell the house (as of 1986), but unless there were new employment opportunities that may have become the only option.

Although the impression of the UC Quarters was fairly good by and large, there was some variation as to housing and the general living standard. The best-equipped house in the area belonged to a household in which the man had been to the Middle East three times and subsequently invested in a private business after having completed his large, well-furnished house. At the other end of the scale were the nonmigrating households and some Middle East households in which the families, for various reasons, had not had the possibility of improving the living standard in any visible sense. The reasons varied—circumstances as to payment conditions in the Gulf, wasteful disposition by the receiver of the money at home or simply the fact that there were too many people in the household to support and nothing was left after daily consumption.

The situation in May Street and Mariya Road was different from the UC Quarters in the sense that at first glance the whole area looked much poorer (with some striking exceptions). Houses were more modest and often not as well equipped as in the UC Quarters. Both May Street and Mariya Road started sending migrants to the Middle East at a later stage than did the UC Quarters. Whereas from the beginning the UC Quarters people did not have to pay large sums to obtain a contract and therefore did not have to get into a new heavy debt before migrating, the latecomers in May Street and Mariya Road faced a different situation.

A striking feature of the development of the migration pattern more or less all over Sri Lanka is that it has become a flourishing business for some people, particularly for illegal agents and, as a consequence, for moneylenders. As the UC Quarters people had gotten into the system when smaller amounts were required to establish a contract, they could more easily continue going through their own networks the second and third times. By the time May Street and Mariya Road entered the scene, agent fees of Rs 3,000–5,000 per contract were common. Most of the people from these communities were already in debt for other reasons before even thinking of a Middle East contract. Consequently very few were able to raise such large sums without borrowing even more. At this point the local moneylenders, came in with ready capital, which was (and is) easy to get if one had personal credibility with the lender and was prepared to pay 20% interest per month. Usually a contract in the Gulf was a good enough guarantee in these transactions.

It is important to note in this context that moneylenders had a strong, well-established position in the area long before the Middle East traffic started. Communities have traditionally been heavily dependent on these moneylenders because of the great variations in income possibilities. This is particularly true with fishing, as there are long periods each year where it is impossible to fish. Hardly any of these poor people had access to regular bank loans, owing to lack of credibility. Consequently having good contacts with moneylenders has been a vital asset for these people, a condition that has led to an immense power position for some of the most successful lenders. This position is reflected in the extremely high interest level demanded and levied.

The majority of the people in these two streets had obtained such loans before going to the Middle East. Obviously this new situation has created a very unequal basis for saving and spending in May Street and Mariya Road as compared to the UC Quarters. At the same time more people in these two streets were actually still working despite having a household member in the Gulf. More people were still fishing "when possible." Such statements, however, are somewhat uncertain, as some men say that they are fishing although they may not have been out in a boat the past ten months. Almost all the households in the area have made some attempts at fishing, but the remuneration has probably not been sufficient for subsistence. When the Middle East option appeared, the income from the sea often did not seem to warrant the effort at all. Consequently many fishermen have withdrawn completely from their former activity and receive a monthly check from their wives instead. An interesting difference between the communities was that some of the men in May Street and Mariya Road expressed a wish to buy fishing equipment with the Gulf money after having improved their houses. In the UC Quarters no one seemed to have any faith whatsoever in future prospects for fishing.

In May Street and Mariya Road, as in the UC Quarters, every household expressed a wish to go to the Middle East as many times as they could manage it. Only two households had not had anyone abroad; the reason was no one to take care of children. True, the husband may have been there, and without any permanent job opportunity, but ascribed gender roles probably rule out this change of responsibility. In such cases there may well be other reasons that household members are not ready to tell outsiders.

As stated, the general impression was of a relatively low standard in these two fishermen's streets. Most people were in the process of improving their houses, though, and the respondents almost invariably stated that they wanted to invest in house improvements as soon as they could afford to.

Two striking exceptions to the living standard were found in the area. These two households had built big brick houses (three to four rooms) that were also well furnished and equipped with a remarkable quantity of expensive trinkets and electric gear (kitchen gadgets, TV sets, radios). These households proved to have two and three daughters in the Gulf, respectively. Especially the house with three daughters abroad seemed to have a well-planned economy, with a father taking care of all "business matters" concerning the daughters' work. The father himself was not working. The purpose now, after having improved the house, was to save a solid dowry for the three daughters. The girls should not go more than twice, according to the father, so as not to spoil their chances on the marriage market. Such rare households would be extremely interesting to visit in five years' time to see where the daughters had moved socially and geographically and to see the living standard of the parents. Dowry saving can be an investment in a true sense for the whole household, as a married daughter will normally support her parents if possible.

As reflected in the discussions above, people in Hambantota also give high priority to housing, if they can afford it when money has been spent on food, clothes, schooling and, quite frequently, "men's spare-time spendings." Differences between the communities concerning housing have been noted. When asked about possible avenues of investment apart from housing, very few mentioned fishing, for reasons already mentioned. "Some business" is the usual answer (from the husbands primarily). In principle the urban setting provides some opportunities in trading. This niche is, however, extremely narrow, and it is hard to make a living as a small-scale trader. Other productive investment usually requires far more capital than can normally be raised through female migration. One avenue that is difficult to investigate, owing to its sensitive character, is the moneylending business. Some informants indicated that some of the migrant households had entered this field on a small scale and that it had been fairly successful. Even though a few people can succeed in this trade, this niche obviously cannot accommodate everyone.

Among all the communities the similarities in trinkets are more striking than the differences. The same gadgets and other items found in Colombo were also prevalent in Hambantota, with a few exceptions. In the Muslim households wall hangings from Mecca were very common. As mentioned, some women even got to go to Mecca while in the Gulf, accompanying their employers. This privilege most likely causes some strange vibrations in the paternalistic Muslim households, as the man of the house can barely dream of a trip to that holy place.

Two Non-fishing Villages in Hambantota

The two control villages will be discussed only to the extent that there are dissimilarities from the fishing communities. One village, located close to the township of Hambantota, used to live primarily from shena cultivation and from some formal employment in salt manufacturing. Households that had depended on shena were facing a more insecure situation, as this pattern of cultivation has become illegal and also difficult to carry out because of the diminishing resource base. Among these households the behavioural pattern related to Middle East migration was very similar to that of the township communities in every aspect that was possible to check. In households in which a male member had permanent employment, the situation was significantly different. These houses looked like middle-class homes of an even higher standard than those in the UC Quarters. The first generation migrant houses of this category were also very well furnished and equipped. The men had all continued their jobs while the wife was in the Gulf. Compared to the overall situation in the township communities this arrangement provides a dual advantage: The household has a permanent income as a basis (even though much lower than the Middle East pay), and there is less likelihood that the husband will squander the remittances. If these households can keep the employment in the future, their possibilities of having a fairly safe economy are good even if the women stop migrating. The shena-based households, however, will probably face the same kinds of problems as the fishing families after a while.

The inland rural Muslim village was originally a settlement scheme from the late 1950s in which each household got a two-room government house and three acres of nonirrigated paddy land. Many of the households were still carrying out shena cultivation. In this fairly remote area women started going to work in the Middle East in 1980. The traffic was introduced through a subagent. Of the nearly 60 households approximately 60% sent one or more women to the Gulf. Very few households had actually managed to improve their housing, even though they had a relatively good starting point in the government houses. This community had also become heavily dependent on moneylenders, who often had taken over some or all of the paddy land the households had originally received through the scheme. Most households had used the remittances for daily consumption and for repaying debts. Everybody expressed a need to go to the Middle East more than once.

In this village one case deviated from the general pattern. This was a Sinhala household in the midst of Muslim homes, and it was well-off by any standard. The family had land, cattle, three fairly big houses and a nice garden with flowers. Two daughters were in the Middle East. Their father however, did not want to talk much about it, as he found it a strange decision on their part. He did not like the fact that they were working in other people's homes, and he did not receive any money from them. The daughters had wanted to go to save for their own futures.

As stated earlier, the similarities between the Hambantota fishing and nonfishing communities are many. Since these rural Muslims had been caught in the vicious circles of poverty for many years and consequently had lost their land and become heavily indebted, the new source of remuneration merely served to keep the daily economy going. Better-off paddy farmers (predominantly Sinhalese) generally seemed very reluctant to participate in the Middle East migration, which they find degrading and basically improper. This attitude may change, however, if it gradually becomes more common among these groups to look for new sources of income.

Gallegama Village

In a paddy area a few miles north of the coastal town of Tangalle in Hambantota District is a small Muslim village that is dealt with as a separate case study. In many respects this little village illustrates some of the more extreme consequences of the Middle East traffic.

Most of the women were still abroad during my visit, so the interviews were undertaken with other family members, primarily the father or husband. These data are consequently not of the same kind as the systematized sample of 139 returned women, and they will be handled in a more qualitative way to underscore some of the phenomenal sides of the migration.

Gallegama (not its real name) is a rural village. It is physically very dense, the 25 houses being situated next to each other without much space in between. The village consists mainly of one curving road with most of the houses on either side. Gallegama is a Muslim island in the midst of Sinhala paddy farmers, making it both physically and culturally somewhat isolated. The first settlers came to Gallegama about sixty-five years ago to work as day labourers in the surrounding paddy fields. A few of them also leased some land occasionally. The economic basis of the village was limited and strongly dependent on the Sinhala paddy farmers. As the village grew in size over the years with very few of its members moving away, the source of income was hardly sufficient for subsistence. In the 1970s almost all the households depended on food stamps to survive. Almost all the families lived in cadjan huts, with little or no plumbing.

Then in 1979 a recruiting agent came to the village, and the first woman left for the Gulf the year after. By 1986, when this field study was undertaken, all but two households had sent at least one woman abroad, and the visual signs of the Middle East traffic were striking. Entering the village, the visitor can be led to think that the inhabitants lead comfortable middle-class lives based on some thriving business: The village road is lined with big (five to seven rooms), expensive whitewashed brick houses with tiled roofs and woodwork attached to doors and windows. This first impression changes, however, when one enters the houses and finds out more of the life stories of the households.

In a small secluded village like Gallegama the demonstration effect of the first returnees is likely to be significant. In Gallegama the first woman to leave had a fairly successful stay in the Gulf, in that she was paid according to contract (standard level), stayed with a family who treated her in such a way that she could endure the whole two-year contract period, and not least, she had a husband who handled the money carefully. Her husband continued his odd jobs while she was away and at least paid for some of the daily household needs. Consequently almost all the Middle East remittances could go into housebuilding. After her first contract the main skeleton of the five-room house was finished. However, no money was left. Consequently the incentive to go on a new contract was strong. After only a few months at home, the wife was off again.

Meanwhile the success of this household encouraged other women to go, as the demand from the Middle East side through local agents only increased. The first household had set the standard concerning how to spend the money: almost all the "petro-dollar houses" had at least five rooms with tiled roofs.

Not all contracts are successful, however, and other circumstances may limit the possibilities of spending vast sums on one project. Consequently many of the second generation migrant houses were started on the basis of unrealistic ambitions. Quite a number of the big houses were not completed, and almost without exception the houses were empty. Even the fortunate households did not have money left for furniture; and the whole village was devoid of all the small trinkets and gadgets so conspicuously present in almost all other migrant communities throughout Sri Lanka. The level of ambition also implied that one contract was enough just to get started. Most households had already sent their women at least twice. Two women were in the Gulf for the third time, and one for the fourth. Some of the households were also sending more than one member at the same time (wife and daughter or two daughters). This practice depended by and large on the number of female members in the house, as there always had to be one fairly grown-up woman at home to take care of the house and the other family members.

Apart from house construction Gallegama Muslims also spent their Middle East money on less visible items. Like other migrant communities in Sri Lanka the households have improved their general standard concerning food consumption and clothing. Most households had made a substantial leap forward from being food-stamp receivers eating mainly rice to a diet where even fish and meat now figured. Almost all the migrant houses said that their standard of living had improved after the Middle East traffic started. In addition to this expenditure most of the migrants had paid the recruiting agent a fee, ranging from Rs 2,000–4,000. To pay it, many were forced to take up loans by local moneylenders, as was the case in Hambantota. The interest rate in Gallegama was 15-20% per month.

What, then, does this tell us? What are the consequences of introducing Gallegama to the Middle East niche of the economy? What is the rationale of the pattern of spending of the inhabitants, and what is the likely viability of the achieved standard of living?

As mentioned, when the traffic started in 1980 the economic basis of the community was probably pressed to the limit, at least in terms of local options. The population had more than doubled since the village had been established without any expansion in land or employment possibilities. The Middle East option obviously was introduced as a safety valve in a rather desperate situation. These circumstances probably explain in part why the village readily responded to this possibility when it appeared. One might otherwise have expected more reluctance from a traditional and secluded Muslim community; only a few of the men had ever travelled beyond the borders of the district, let alone the women, who were strictly controlled by the head of household.

Once the migration got started, other households followed suit, owing at least in part to the market demonstration effect of the pioneers. Concerning priorities one can say that this village has, with some qualification as to invisible spendings on food and interest, put all its eggs into one basket—house-building. To judge whether this reflects wise economic planning, or rather to uncover what economic rationale lies behind this practice, we need to discuss the choices available to the village.

In the first place, building a solid waterproof house makes sense in itself when one lives in a one-room cadjan hut with a family of eight to ten people. Besides, and probably most important, there are not many (if any) avenues for investment available. It is impossible to buy land in the surrounding area, as the relatively well-off Sinhala paddy-growers are not willing to sell away property. The wider area is rural, of low population density and without many possibilities for investment in trading or other activities. Nevertheless, one may obviously question the rationale of building five-to-seven-room houses that may not be completed and that in consequence limit the possibilities of establishing some financial security for the future, if only through a bank account. This point is underscored even more strongly when we look into future scenarios for Gallegama.

The demand for Muslim Sri Lankan women in the Middle East is fairly stable, so Gallegama women may be able to continue migrating for some more years to come. We are not looking into the possible detrimental effects on family life, reproduction and the woman herself, only at the economic consequences. If the traffic is to continue for, say, another ten years, there is also likely to be a physical and social limit for each and every woman migrating on two-year contracts.

However, there are indications that the Gulf traffic will not last for an unlimited number of years. The demand for domestic servants has been strongly conditioned by the oil boom that is possibly fading out. At present the whole economy of Gallegama is dependent on incomes from the Middle East. (The only two households without anyone with Middle East experience were still receiving food stamps. They were extremely poor households, without a male breadwinner and without anyone to take care of the children to enable the adult woman to go on contract.) The majority of households have no stable work besides the Gulf employment. Moreover, what employment many of the men do have is also closely linked to the Gulf traffic, such as assisting neighbors in housebuilding.

In view of the grim prospects for the local economy as to alternative employment, the pretentious housebuilding leaves us with a gloomy picture. Even though the citizens of Gallegama have been much more rational in economic terms than have many of the migrants elsewhere in Sri Lanka—not squandering money on alcohol and lotteries—their rationale may prove disastrous in the end. If and when the Middle East money dries up, they will be left with big, expensive houses worth very little on the market, owing to the limited economic base in the area; they probably will not have saved enough money to establish themselves elsewhere (if indeed that option exists); and the possibilities of some local employment will be even worse than before. In addition, it is not likely that they will be reenrolled as food stamp receivers because of their showy houses.

I have devoted so much space to the case of Gallegama because it illustrates the contradictory sides of the labour migration. On the one hand, the traffic is a survival strategy that may in fact be quite lucrative, relatively speaking, if the conditions from the outset permit and if some economic planning is present. On the other hand, it may create a dependency trap from which there is no easy escape. Much depends on the sustainability of the female migration. Most households in Gallegama, when asked what they would give priority to after finishing their houses, answered "children's education" and then "future savings." It is an open question whether they will ever reach this second stage.

Spending Patterns in Colombo and Hambantota

I have so far handled Colombo and Hambantota separately concerning observations and interviews in the field. In this brief section I present the general pattern in the two areas, as to the economic effects (spending pattern) of migration. The figures from Hambantota and Colombo are again combined in the cases in which variation is insignificant. A few references to the national surveys are given. When variation is apparent, Colombo and Hambantota are treated separately.

The majority of the women (80%) remitted their earnings regularly to their households at home, and of these 59% sent money monthly. A smaller majority (56%) of the maids remitted more or less everything they earned, usually with the exception of the last three or four months' salary to buy goods to bring home. The national data show that women generally remitted a greater part of their wages than did male migrants (67% of the total earnings were sent home during the contract period by female migrants [Korale et al., 1985]). According to the Marga findings, women remit 87% of their Middle East money, whereas men remit only 58%.

Of the sample 43% sent a check to the husband when money was remitted. Thus a fairly large group of the married migrants did not find it convenient to use the husband as a receiver. The reason for this may be practical, although the impression given is that the migrant felt other household members (usually the caretaker of the children) could be trusted to a greater degree when it came to handling money to the benefit of the family.[2]

Gulf money was spent on a whole range of items and activities, although a certain pattern can be identified across the communities. A good house has high status in the communities, and the great majority said they wanted to spend as much as possible on improving or rebuilding the house. When it comes to the ability to realize this desire fully or partly, the picture varies greatly: 48% were not able to spend anything on housing at all. In fact, variation between the areas proved to be fairly small. (See Table 7.1.)

Concerning the outcome of the Gulf contracts, we might expect somewhat different patterns in Colombo compared to Hambantota, due to the different economic basis and, to a certain degree, housing standard at the outset. Since people in Hambantota almost invariably wanted to stay in the same community (whereas the Colombo dwellers more than anything wanted to escape the slum), we would expect that the incentive to improve their living standard on the site would be greater in Hambantota.

Interestingly in Hambantota there are rather few households in the middle of the scale. Either they invested hardly anything, or they spent significant amounts. This finding suggests that the majority have scarcely anything left over for solid investments or else that they belong to better-off groups with another economic basis and so can pool most of the external remittances for the housing improvements. These figures must also be seen in contrast to other expenditures. In Hambantota there was

TABLE 7.1 Amount of Female Migrants' Earnings Spent on Improving Housing Standard, Colombo Compared to Hambantota

Spending (Rs)	*Colombo*	*Hambantota*	*Total %*
0	51	37	48
1–10,000	24	14	23
10,001–15,000	8	–	7
15,001–20,000	3	–	2
20,001–35,000	4	26	8
35,000+	11	23	19
Total %	101	100	100
N	110	27	137

altogether not much higher propensity to buy things (kitchen gadgets, cassette players, TV sets, trinkets, and so on) than in Colombo (52% versus 50%). (See Table 7.2.) In terms of actual expenditure, however, there was a difference: 30% of the Hambantota sample had spent more than Rs 3,000 on such products (Colombo, 6%).

The usual pattern in both places was to buy at least some inevitable items like a cassette player, fancy toys and at least one wristwatch for the father or husband. Here it is hard to sketch a systematic picture on the basis of the data collected in Hambantota. The only systematic (to the extreme) example in this respect is the village Gallegama, which I have discussed at length.

According to the Marga data, 54% of all female migrants were able to invest in housing at some level, and 38% of all the money remitted by the maids was used on housing. The Korale investigation reveals that the average spending in this context is Rs 7,200.

The income strategies that form the basis for the household economies are, as we have seen, somewhat different in Colombo compared to Hambantota. In Hambantota, naturally, people have closer contact with productive bases like agriculture and fishing than in the big city, although the differences are growing smaller. On the other hand, in Colombo there are, despite the narrow niches and the economic crisis, more possibilities in the informal sector. This difference is not reflected in the figures on *investment,* however, in terms of production, business or any

TABLE 7.2 Amount of Female Migrants' Earnings Spent on Status Symbols, Colombo Compared to Hambantota

Rs. Spent	*Colombo*	*Hambantota*	*Total %*
0	50	52	50
1–1,000	31	7	26
1,001–1,500	8	–	7
1,501–3,000	5	11	6
3,001+	6	30	11
Total %	100	100	100
N	110	27	137

other activity that can promote an income independently of the migration.

As we can see in Table 7.3, the percentage who actually invest is strikingly low; nearly 95% of the sample did not undertake any form of such investments. (According to Marga, only 2% invested at all.) As previously mentioned, gold is the kind of merchandise that comes closest to an investment, as it can be used as dowry for unmarried women in the household. Even here only 51% spend money on gold, and by and large the amounts are low. Only 7% of the sample report having saved money for dowry either for themselves or for a relative. Altogether 82% did not have any money left themselves when they returned to Sri Lanka after terminating the contract.

A central variable for economic consequences of female migration is the work status of the husband, particularly when the wife is abroad. This variable forms an important premise for the economic behaviour of the head of household in relation to female migration. (See Table 7.4.) The category "no job" means actually unemployed, whereas "retreated" implies that the husband actively pulled out of the labour market when the wife left (or some time afterwards). The dividing line between "retreated" and "job as usual" is fairly vague, however, as many men may report that they worked as they used to, although the activity rate could have been much lower. This reservation applies mostly to work within the informal sector, where the activity rate as well as the salary are not easy to estimate. The high percentage for "job as usual" in Hambantota can be somewhat misleading. As a high proportion of the sample belonged to fishing communities, it is hard to assess what is actual work and what is potential work. Fishing is at best an unstable

TABLE 7.3 Investments Made by Female Migrants

Amount Invested (Rs)	*N*	*%*
0	131	95
1–5,000	2	1
5,001–12,000	2	1
12,000+	3	2
	138	99
		2 NI

TABLE 7.4 Husband's Job Status While Maid Is in the Gulf, Colombo Compared to Hambantota

Job Status	*Colombo*	*Hambantota*	*Total %*
No job	38	18	34
Retreated		15	15
Job as usual	47	71	52
Total %	100	101	101
N	72	17	89

occupation, and many men still call themselves fishermen even though they do not actually fish. The statement "job as usual" is obviously dubious when "fishing" sometimes meant going out twice a year even before the women left.

What emerges clearly from this data is that the majority of the households spend the lion's share of the earnings on daily consumption. To evaluate how the consumption pattern has changed through migration, we would need a well-defined profile of the pattern prior to migration. Although such data are lacking, the Marga report estimates that general household consumption has increased two and one-half times because of the Middle East jobs and that the households spend on average Rs 1,800 per month while money is remitted.

Even though the majority clearly improve their level of daily consumption through the Middle East migration, 43% of the sample stated that they have the same standard of living as before (51% reported "better" and 5% "worse"). Although a fairly large part of the remittances may be squandered in some households, objectively the figure must be wrong. Subjectively, however, it may feel the same if the material surroundings are the same, and nothing is left of the money after terminating the contract.

Of the sample 51% stated that they felt the money had been used in a fairly acceptable manner; 28% thought that the remittances had been used wisely; and 21%, badly.

As mentioned, 80% of the sample wanted to go on another contract if the possibility were there. The pattern of priority concerning spending avenues (apart from daily consumption) in case of new trips to the Gulf, is shown in Tables 7.5 and 7.6. The tables show first and second priorities if the women could choose freely between different options.

A quite large part of the group still gave high priority to housing, both as first and second priority (33% and 28%, respectively). The second highest category as first priority is to "buy land." This response applies almost exclusively to the Colombo sample—people who want to escape the slum areas. Children's education scores fairly high as a second priority, once the household has established the material standard at a higher level. A substantial increase is observed in the category "save" from first to second priorities (15% to 36%). This finding implies that when people feel that they have made major investments, particularly in housing, they find it wise to save for the future. A strikingly low proportion of the sample saw any prospect for investing in any lasting economic activity.

Dispositional Effects: Microlevel Conclusions

Considering the "dispositional effects"—that is, how the money is used—various factors play a part. That hardly anyone in the households has a stable income implies that the Middle East salary will often represent the only money worth mentioning for these families. As we have seen, not infrequently other family members will stop whatever work they were doing because the money does not seem to be worth the effort in view of the Middle East contribution that arrives every month. The number of consumers in the household therefore increases, and the need for leisure activities arises. It is not unusual (although to varying degrees) for the women to find upon their return that their Gulf wages have been squandered on alcohol, gambling or other dubious undertakings while they were away. A general feature in these communities is lack of financial stability. Most households cite "various odd jobs" as the financial basis of the family. They are generally not

TABLE 7.5 First Priority of Female Migrants in Case of a New Contract in the Gulf

First Priority	*N*	%
Not going	5	4
Improve house	45	33
Education/children	11	8
Save money	20	15
Buy land	39	28
Invest	2	1
Dowry	16	12
	138	101
		2 NI

TABLE 7.6 Second Priority of Female Migrants in Case of a New Contract in the Gulf

Second Priority	*N*	%
Not going		8
Improve house	38	28
Education/children	25	18
Save		36
Invest	4	3
Dowry	11	8
	138	101
		2 NI

used to having money, and whatever money is occasionally available has been spent immediately. Budgetary planning has hardly existed, first and foremost because there has not been anything to plan on. Consequently the behaviour of these families should be of no surprise. Indeed, it is instead rather striking that so many do manage to save enough to rebuild their houses.

Literature on labour migration often features the concept of "conspicuous consumption." This phrase refers to a consumption pattern characteristic of the nouveau riche, in which cassette players, TV sets, extravagant furniture, bric-a-brac and trinkets dominate. Such visual signs of the Middle East migration are also found in Sri Lanka, although usually to a modest degree. Very few of these women have returned without a cassette player, toys for the children, a wristwatch for the husband or a number of saris for themselves. There is a possibility also that the maids are somewhat influenced by the luxurious standard of living they experience in the Gulf as to the things they buy upon their return; electric kitchen utensils, for example, would probably not have been high on the priority list otherwise.

Nevertheless, we should be careful in drawing conclusions. The data in this study indicate that the great majority spend the bulk of their wages on (1) repaying debts, (2) daily consumption, (3) improvements in the house, (4) more expensive status symbols.[3] The ranking between (3) and (4) may vary. Relatively more money is needed to improve the housing standard, so that if a woman or a household does not see the possibility of passing this threshold, status symbols may get higher priority.[4]

The rationale behind this pattern needs some comment. The wage level in the Middle East is so high that we might have expected a stronger propensity to invest—more wise, long-term thinking that could contribute to pulling the actors out of the worst poverty. Investments in some financial activities ("business"), which in turn could yield a basis independent of the Gulf traffic, would be an expression of such thinking. That this happens only rarely has in part to do with the initial resources and the vicious circles discussed earlier. The standard of living is from the outset so low that spending on better food, health, clothing and housing obviously makes sense.[5] If there is then any money left, one can ask whether it is wise to invest or save under the prevailing circumstances. One limitation is lack of objects for investment at the financial level of the people in question. Niches in the informal sector are already overcrowded, which is one reason the need to migrate arose in the first place. On the other hand, some of the gadgets that the migrants do spend money on—like TV sets, gold and houses—may at least in principle be an asset that the household can later sell, and as such they represent an investment in economic security.

Education is a long-term investment, traditionally highly valued in Sri Lanka, and education is also one area most people say they want to spend money on. The financial return of this investment is not within direct view, though; and indeed the direct financial value of education has generally been deflated in recent years.

A somewhat special kind of investment, dependent to a limited degree on the initial resources, is collecting a dowry for the migrant herself, if she is not married, or for close female family members. The dowry system is still fairly widespread in the country, and marrying above one's station may yield financial returns for other family members as well. According to the present sample, however, this investment is not frequent among the housemaids.

One should probably broaden the concept of investment somewhat, differentiating between investment in the pecuniary meaning of the word, as we have discussed it so far, and investment in local status. It is fairly common among the migrants to spend money on weddings, funerals, age attainment and village festivals in a more conspicuous way than before going abroad. Symbolic treasures may definitely have value as such, and they may also be transferred into more solid assets.

These investments in status should also be viewed in a broader class context. As has already been seen, middle-class values have a predominate position in Sri Lankan society and have percolated down to even the lowest social layers through the press and through demonstration effects in various fields over the years. Before the new migrant wave started at the beginning of the 1980s, migration and travelling to distant places had been an upper- and middle-class phenomenon. Sending things home from abroad had been related to high status, both for the sender and the receiver. The show-off tendencies that the new migrants sometimes embark on should be appraised in this context. These manifestations of status among the new migrants naturally contribute in turn to the reproduction of the pull factors among prospective migrants and intermingle with the economic motivation of improving the daily living standard of the family.

Village Sri Lanka, being a fairly egalitarian society in which comparison with the neighbors is a central feature, spending behaviour tends to follow specific patterns according to local definitions of status.[6] For years, housing has held a significant position in this context. As discussed previously, the core-family concept has had a high standing in Sri Lankan society over the years, and acquiring a private home for the closest kin seems to be the most prominent aspiration expressed by almost everybody in the villages studied. This phenomenon has also been explained in class terms in Chapter 2. It is therefore not surprising that improving or rebuilding the family house has such a high priority when more money becomes available.[7]

At least in the first stages of a migration flow, it seems natural to find traditionally familiar objects among the spending priorities. (See also Dias, 1983.) After a longer period of migration, though, this pattern may be extended or redefined through "pioneer behaviour" and subsequent demonstration effect.

There are altogether very few mobile maids who actually reach the stage of investing their wages in the narrow, pecuniary way, at least so far. Many women have been to the Middle East up to three times without breaking out of the consumption trap. A "family-supporter logic" has by necessity come to direct the female migrants and their households, and high levels of consumption have in turn made them dependent on a series of new contracts in the Gulf. As in many other sender economies labour migration and higher aspirations tend to be mutually reinforced.

For many households it will be impossible to keep sending their women abroad for years and years. Neither is it likely that the demand will be eternal. The long-term effects for the households that use the Middle East money primarily for subsistence are grim. A new dependency is created, although on a higher consumption level. Consequently it seems that the strategic variable to get off the ground in a lasting sense is a permanent income in the household (not necessarily very large) apart from the Middle East salary. This requirement is important also as some permanence in relation to the economic situation seems correlated to a sense of economic planning. The mentality in such households is likely to be very different from, for example, the fishing households that are used to living from day to day.

Another strategic variable is size of household. Having too many dependents certainly poses constraints on the economy. However, having more daughters of a suitable age for migration has proven a major asset for a family. More than one Middle East income at the same time may give the extra leverage to provide the family with a more lasting uplift.

Consequently the possibilities provided by work in the Middle East have had contradictory implications on the household economies of the maids. On the one hand, they have enhanced most households' spending capacities and hence improved their living conditions, at least in the short run. On the other hand, opportunity cost has greatly increased as to other income-generating activities for all household members. The relative futility of engaging in other income-generating activities for the men in particular has been noted in this respect. Their efforts will not easily be seen to be warranted in the context of the monthly petro-dollar cheques arriving from abroad.

Thus the constraints are many throughout the migration process. Nevertheless, for thousands of women the structural driving forces, as well as the various facilitators in society, still outweigh these constraints when it comes to the actual move. On the result side it may be the other way around, in that various barriers in society make it exceedingly difficult to transcend poverty, despite the Gulf money.

Notes

1. This scene has changed drastically in the period since the fieldwork was undertaken. Hambantota District has been strongly affected by the political turmoil in the wake of the ethnic conflict of the island in the late 1980s.

2. In the Colombo-Leiden survey (Eelens, Schampers and Speckmann, 1991), out of a sample of 676 housemaids, 64.5% said that nothing had been saved by the family back home at the time of return.

3. By "status symbols" is meant gadgets that serve primarily the purpose of demonstrating "success" or "prosperity." This is not to say that some of the other dispositions (like housebuilding) may not also contain such status aspects.

4. Lack of solid investments seems to be a fairly widespread phenomenon in the context of labour migration. Demery (1986) has shown that typically 50–70% of remittances in Asia go to daily consumption, and only 10% will be invested (Demery, 1986).

5. Even though health care is supposed to be free in Sri Lanka, people who have money (however little) tend to give high priority to better health care than what they are offered for free.

6. The local priority pattern according to symbolic status may also be influenced by caste issues. This study has not disclosed any variation in this respect (as the priorities seemed fairly uniform), a fact that does not necessarily mean that caste aspects are insignificant. Caste-related questions are complicated and time consuming to

uncover, however, and have not been a central concern of this investigation.

7. This phenomenon seems to be fairly widespread in the context of labour migration. Nermin Abadan-Unat (1984) talks about a "Separate-house-in-the-village-syndrome" in this respect.

8

Consequences of Female Migration to the Middle East

I have noted how the main intention of Sri Lanka's female migrants—economic benefit to improve the living standard of their families—is fulfilled only to a fairly small extent. On the basis of data presented in previous chapters, I will wind up by analyzing the cumulative processes involved whereby combinations of barriers and constraints serve to undermine initial intentions. In other words, I will discuss whether the preconditions for the original decisionmaking have been undermined in the process. I will also discuss whether there are other more symbolic or status-related aspects being fulfilled through the job abroad, contributing to a richer understanding of the post-migration behaviour and the reproduction of the pull forces, relatively apart from the economic realm. The various problems raised earlier in the study related to the major ideological barriers in society—religious/cultural norms and sex roles—will be discussed in terms of impact on gender relations and reduced subordination.

Impact on Gender Relations, Micro and Macro

The social and cultural impact of labour migration is less well documented than the economic consequences. Some studies in sender countries have linked migration to sociocultural developments like changes in the status of women, family relationships (including marital stability and age of marriage), psychological problems of children, educational aspirations and so on. Almost all of the studies, however, are linked to male migration, and the interlinkages between the different dimensions have not been developed very far. These limitations could be due partly to the substance of the field. It is probably even more difficult to control for other factors in this field than concerning remittances, and the data cannot easily be substantiated in a quantitative way. To undertake comprehensive studies, one would need longitudinal data, which are not usually available.

I have already focused on the more striking gender aspects of the female migration—women crossing borders in a double sense. Even though the decision to go abroad to work is gradually becoming less drastic culturally and socially as more and more women go, the act that the individual woman undertakes and the experience of the stay remain a fundamental step for the woman herself. Also, these are women who have been far beyond the daily control of their husbands for a long period; and not least, they have become financially important, almost indispensable, for their households.

Female migration from Sri Lanka to the Gulf is a recent phenomenon, which means that an appraisal of the long-term, lasting impact cannot yet be undertaken, particularly since the transformation of social norms—gender norms in this case—represents a very slow process. To understand these processes in depth, a series of long-term anthropological studies would be required, in which ethnic, religious, caste and class differences would be incorporated into the gender issue. As yet no such study has been done, a fact that creates some problems of scientific evidence. It is, possible, however, to hypothesize the long-term effects, based on an assessment of general traits of society, the observed short-term effects and experiences from comparable cases elsewhere.

Major social changes are usually accompanied by strains and conflicts, and disturbances in the traditional gender-role system are no exception. However, in the case of the female migration we have also noted certain ambiguities as to the prominence of the substantial changes taking place. These ambiguities are related to both the kind of work the women do and to the persistence of the traditional social organization in the areas of origin.

On the one hand, the women undertake work that is considered low-grade in a context in which they are often severely exploited and/or badly treated. On the other hand, they are remunerated at a significantly better rate than they themselves and their men can dream of at home. They have also proven themselves geographically mobile to an unprecedented degree. Not least important is the fact that this wage work takes place in a context in which their men's economic position is deteriorating simultaneously.

I have earlier (Chapter 1) placed the household as the basic unit generating gender inequality in society by analyzing the nature of redistribution processes within the unit. The major points of this analysis can be summed up as follows: The household is somehow a collective decisionmaking unit, although basically not a democratic or egalitarian one. Central decisions on consumption, production, fertility, marriage and migration are made according to the traditional patriarchal structure of the household. The interests of the individuals in the household do not necessarily coincide with those of the collective. Not all members benefit equally from courses of action taken by individual household members. Nor do household members pool their income and allocate resources according to principles of economic rationality of the collective. On the contrary, it is increasingly demonstrated that asymmetrical exchanges along gender and age lines within households produce and reify hierarchies of inequality (Tienda and Booth, 1988).

Women have for ages contributed to the household economy in the context of poor Sri Lankan communities. The major change in the 1980s is that this contribution was monetized to a much greater degree. At the same time money has become increasingly important in the general household economy. Against this background, the question is whether the new situation has significantly increased the bargaining power of women in relation to their close surroundings, implying in turn an enhancement of their social position. In other words, does female migration serve to undermine patriarchal authority in their households and in the close community?

An operationalization of this broad question is necessary. One of the most important indicators of relative power position in the household is budget control. As D. Kandiyoti has stated, it cannot be concluded that access to income and budget control are one and the same thing (Kandiyoti, 1988).

Budget Control

Men's misbehaviour and wasteful spending while the women are away is a commonly heard complaint among the women themselves, their relatives and their neighbors. Very often men who at least used to have some income, whether from fishing or various odd jobs, withdraw completely from income-earning activities when the wife leaves. This reaction does not usually apply when the man has some sort of stable employment. In a way, this can be sensible behaviour, in view of the imbalance between efforts they make and the remuneration. Scarcely any available male earning in the neighborhood could even approach the level of the Gulf salaries. Provided that the women send their husbands a monthly check (also the pattern in Hambantota), the likelihood that the men sit back doing very little is high. If the men are into the habit of drinking, this obviously adds another constraint on the family budget. This behavior sometimes leads to a situation in which the wife finds that very little is left for savings or investment when she returns after two years. That such a situation leads to severe disagreement between the spouses is not surprising. It also reemphasizes the need to go on another contract quite soon.

When asked about budget aspects and spending priorities, quite a number of the women in the study answered that they themselves made the decisions together with the husband or father.[1] Since the spending pattern often indicates that it is not the woman (or the children) who benefit first, such answers have to be scrutinized more thoroughly. There are basically two possible interpretations: One is that the women do participate in the decision but that they choose to comply with the view of the man because they think he is right. The other interpretation is that they are simply overruled directly or subtly. Both alternatives may be present, depending on the circumstances. In most cases where the woman actually states that the man has used the money in a wise way while she was abroad, the man has rebuilt the house and used money for daily maintenance. This use of the money is most probably what the woman would have chosen herself had she been in direct control of the money, although (sometimes important) details may have been handled differently.[2] However, in most cases the deed to the house is in the name of the man, which means that in case of a divorce the man has the right to the house.[3]

The clearest case in which the woman is directly overruled occurs when she comes home to find that nothing is left of the money and that most of it has been squandered on leisure activities by the husband. The powerlessness of these women becomes even more striking when this scenario is repeated two or three times without the woman's changing the arrangement whereby a monthly check is sent home to the husband. This is not the usual picture, however. Quite a number of the women migrants feel that they have a greater say as to the spending of the household.

Accepting the premises of the traditional communities, we find one example in which the Middle East money is used for the migrant herself when money is put aside for her own dowry. As we have seen, this does not in fact take place to any large degree in the communities studied. However, there are indications that employment as such is slowly coming to replace the old dowry system (De Silva, 1981; Jayaweera, 1979). If this is the case, it is in fact a very significant change that revises the whole concept of dowry: The woman is no longer regarded as only another mouth to feed but is explicitly considered a breadwinner. We should, however, not overemphasize this point in relation to Middle East migration so far. Most communities look upon the traffic as something temporary, at least for individuals; it is not possible to keep sending the same woman for an indefinite number of years, and so far very few Middle East maids have gone into wage work after their return home.

Share of Work and Family Relations

Another indicator of enhanced position in the household would be a true redistribution of the work and responsibilities between the sexes. There are hardly any indications that this is taking place in the wake of female migration so far. During the woman's absence another woman, usually from the close kin group, takes over responsibility for housework and daily care of the family.

In practical terms men rarely take this responsibility. In 73% of the cases (in Colombo and Hambantota) the mother, mother-in-law or sister of the migrant moved into the household (if she did not live there already) to substitute. In 7% of the cases others did this job (usually a daughter or the husband's sister). Although 15% reported that the husband was the caretaker, this figure is probably somewhat high, as a number of people felt that the husband had been responsible for the household although he had not actually done the cooking and the cleaning himself. The husband's work status during the wife's absence is not necessarily correlated with his participation in the household chores. The family would have to be in a desperate situation before the man took over cooking and cleaning. When the migrant returned, the division of labour almost invariably reverted to the old pattern.

One social effect that can be observed seems to be increased interdependence among family members and strengthened extended family networks. This effect seems to be the case throughout much of South and Southeast Asia (see Arnold, 1988; Korale, 1983). In the cases where the eldest daughter in the house has to take mother's place, there may be unfortunate side effects as to the young girl's educational attainment. This example is a clear illustration of how the female networks—based on traditional responsibility in the realm of the family—may yield very diverse results for women at different stages of the life cycle. Daughters' neglect of schooling as a consequence of the mother's absence is sometimes seen as an even wider threat in the realm of girls' moral standards and role attainment. One principal at a girls' school in Colombo was worried that the mothers in the Middle East constituted a model for the girls in that they wanted to start earning money as soon as possible and schoolwork was consequently ignored. Some principals even stated that the young Middle East daughters occasionally went into prostitution.[4]

An expression often heard in relation to labour migration (both male and female) from Asia to the Middle East is the "Dubai syndrome." Even though migration may take a toll on both those who go and those who stay behind, this phrase is by and large used to describe the psychological (and to a certain extent, physical) distress of the family members left behind. Since most studies in this field have focused on male migration, the syndrome is usually applied to the women left behind. Various maladies are cited, such as fatigue, depression, delayed menstruation and generally a series of psychosomatic symptoms, suicide representing the ultimate reaction.

Similar symptoms can be observed in the case of female migration in Sri Lanka, although the most noticeable reactions commonly apply to the children rather than the husbands left behind. Very young children, in particular, seem to suffer from the long absence of their mothers (Eelens and Schampers, 1988). According to estimates made by Eelens and Schampers, there are about 260,000 Sri Lankan children whose mothers are in the Gulf; 200,000 of these children are under ten years old, and 19,000 are said to be under one year of age (1986). The person who takes over the supervision of the household is also subject to substantial stress. The psychology of absenteeism[5] thus affects a number of people when a central person in the household is absent. In some reports migration is even blamed for social ills like drug use and juvenile delinquency, all traced back to the absence of the parent.

On the one hand, family networks help the members left behind to cope reasonably well in the absence of the mother and wife, even though there may often be social tension and conflicts involved in the arrangement. On the other hand, the migrant may be confronted with pressure to help out more distant relatives. Some migrants complained that family ties had strategically been called upon once they had achieved a contract in the Gulf. However, such strengthened kin ties as a result of migration are likely to be of a temporary character, lasting as long as the women actually work abroad. Most families (migrant or husband) mention that the future dream is to have a house just for the nuclear family. At the same time the feeling of responsibility towards one's parents still seems to be a fairly widespread imperative in Sri Lankan society.

Marriage and Role Conflicts

More important as to changes in the family structure in the wake of female migration is probably the impact on the married couple itself. There is obviously a high conflict potential in the system due to the separation in the first place, and second, due to the changes in the economic role pattern of the family. The combination "male unemployment–female breadwinner" does not easily promote harmony in the home. This "domestication of men"[6] may actually generate a tendency to stronger subordination of the woman by her husband as a reaction to threatened male identity. The relative strength of the woman will subsequently determine the outcome of the struggle.

One in-depth interview with a "Middle East husband" in one of the fishing villages in Hambantota illustrates this field. This husband was highly unusual in that he took care of the house and the children by himself. He used to go fishing but had withdrawn completely from this activity to look after the home while the wife was away. In his opinion the female migration had implied drastic changes in the communities, primarily due to all the money that was flowing in. Moneylenders had even better times than they used to. Money had become more important among people than before. Acts of friendship and mutual support had to a large extent changed to money transactions. According to him, people had become much more status conscious, and status was now more strongly linked to what could be bought for money. He felt migration had done a lot of harm to community cohesion, although he could not see any viable alternative at the time, since fishing was hardly worth the effort. This man's opinion as to the gender roles and the husband-wife relationship reflected a strong concern about loss of dignity, "loose behaviour," broken marriages and liberated women. He felt that the Middle East migration had turned upside down many of the traditional values and patterns of behaviour. In more concrete terms only a few marriages in the area had broken up. The reason could be either that the woman "kicked out the man" when she got home (mainly because he had taken another woman in her absence) or simply that she was not satisfied with his behaviour. Such breakups would hardly ever have happened before, according to the source. The general impression was that the women had become more self-assertive, feeling superior in the knowledge that they were the real breadwinners.

These views reflect similar opinions gathered in bits and pieces from other sources in the area. Even though they very likely may be exaggerations of reality, the conception is worth noting. These attitudes imply that a new female character is created, although it may well be a myth. The notion also reflects the perception that even though it may not be true that the women feel superior after a contract in the Gulf, the men feel inferior. Where this will lead in the near and distant future is hard to tell. It is probably not likely that the repercussions will be lasting if this Middle East option proves to be only an intermezzo in their lives. It is also important in this respect to underscore that the marriages and the men's behaviour were not that different before migration started and that, again, it is difficult to isolate one causal factor.

Another interesting feature is that men seem to find returned migrants more attractive on the marriage market even though it is often said that they are "loose" and "spoiled" as women after being out of sight for so long. The image of "what is going on out there" is fairly bad. Again, money is becoming more significant than dignity and tradition when finding a spouse.

According to Korale (1983) the divorce rate is higher among migrant families than control families. Although it is difficult to establish the direct causal relationship between migration and divorce, it intuitively makes sense. There is a basic contradictory exigency in the migration system that impinges on the conjugal relationship: The economic viability of a conjugal association de facto requires the separation of the spouses, whereas such prolonged separation contributes to the undermining of the relationship.[7] However, a crumbling relationship may increase the motivation to stay away for a period of time. Nevertheless, in the Sri Lankan context (and many others as well) the family's survival is in fact almost contingent on this family separation for the time being. The human cost of this separation is very high.

Age of Marriage and Fertility

Data are scarce on the impact migration could have on the age of marriage and fertility. It is a fact, however, that the age of marriage has generally increased in Sri Lankan society since then 1970s. Whereas the average age of marriage for women in 1970 was 23.6 (men, 26.2), by 1981 it had increased to 24.4 (men, 27.2) (Liljestrom, 1983). There can be complex reasons for this tendency. Stronger female wage labour participation is usually believed to be one. This factor obviously applies only to the maids who are not already married (who are in minority), and who may postpone the wedding to secure the financial basis for the family or for themselves. Concerning fertility, there is very likely to be some impact, as most women leave their home for lengthy periods of time during their most fertile years. How significant this impact will be is uncertain. It may imply that the female migrants only postpone the childbearing until after they have stopped going to the Gulf. Whether that is going to influence the total number of children born to the family, however, remains to be seen.

Change in Social Status

The question of "liberation" may under the circumstances seem rather misplaced, both concerning the working conditions in the Gulf and the socioeconomic situation at home. Using the term in the relative sense introduced earlier will nevertheless point to some tendencies as to the improvement or deterioration (or both) of the general social status of the women in question.

In assessing the issue of improved social status, one should take into consideration both the actor and the surrounding structures and the interplay between the two, both in the situation in the Gulf and in the home communities. The serf-like conditions the women usually face abroad, with strong hierarchical social relations, may actually reinforce the conception of gender roles that the women brought with them from home. Even though the move itself reflects a kind of transcendence, the type of experience (the process conditions, including the psychological aspects) they have had in the Gulf will clearly influence the self-confidence of the women. Each woman, then, will return home with her specific experience, which again influences the way she will act in relation to the local structures of behaviour. These structures are, as we have seen, not very conducive to major changes in sex role patterns. The net effect of the whole migration system concerning the social status of the women will in this way depend on the complex interplay between structures and actors at both ends of the chain.

Given these important limitations, this study shows that a substantial number of the maids return home more exhausted than liberated. Maltreatment, hard work and loneliness do not easily promote increased self-esteem and assertiveness. There are, however, examples of women who have achieved a new confidence through their stay abroad, and who—at least for the time being—show a firmness that was not there before.[8] They have gained personal strength by conquering a new world by themselves, enduring pressure and completing the set task in favour of their families back home. These examples are very few, indeed, but they nevertheless reflect that a possibility is there, if the working conditions are good or acceptable and the woman is mentally prepared for the job.

Most studies on effects of female migration seem very hesitant concerning any liberating effect of labour migration. M. Tienda and K. Booth write, for example: "That migrant women's entry into paid employment usually arises because of dire necessity, and leaves patriarchal authority essentially unaltered, puts a brake on the extent to which migration modifies gender relations. . . . Migration results in 'restructured constants' to the extent that gender asymmetries are left intact while only the content of women's activities change as a result of migration" (Tienda and Booth, 1988:310).

Others stress that new forms of gender subordination arise out of the nature of women's integration into wage labour (Heyzer, 1986) or call it "pseudo-emancipation" (Abadan-Unat, 1986). What they are saying is that the traditional ideology catches up with women in the household, either through direct oppressive measures from others or through social power mechanisms that "force the individual back on himself and tie him to his own identity in a constrained way" (Foucault, 1983).

Such pessimism may be justified. In fact, data from this study point in the same direction. Nevertheless, it is important to keep an open mind towards the possibility of slow processes of change not easily tracked down in short-term studies. Over time the symbolic milieu will also change since a substantial group of women migrate. The changes may be subtle, in that women may have a stronger say in decisionmaking processes not visible from outside. The room for maneuvering within the existing frame of reference may have widened without challenging the basic structure in the first round.

All in all, it is difficult to conclude that migration as such promotes a change in women's position, although it permits an opportunity for change by providing a new set of options in their lives. From this study it is clear that women's work as well as their social status are largely directed by broader structural and political systems that limit the possibilities of emancipation for the women involved. These systems institute rules of behaviour by which men and women are obliged to act and interact, and these rules again are embedded in questions of power and control. Nevertheless, migration may act as a long-term catalyst for change in relation to both the labour market and the private sphere.

The female labour migration from Sri Lanka has at least contributed to making women's work for remuneration more visible on the social scene because of the relatively high amounts of money they generate and because of the character of the work, in that they have to leave the country with resulting heavy social costs. As a result of the economic gains in the Middle East, women have become assets to their households. The traffic to the Gulf has also proved that limitations placed on women's physical mobility have been de facto modified.

Final conclusions have yet to be drawn on this question. It seems important not to search for one single conclusion but rather leave room for complex and even apparently contradictory outcomes. The women and the role setup in the households may by and large appear unaltered for the time being. Subtle processes of change may, however, take place under the surface as a consequence of drastic events like this. Visible changes in terms of more equal sharing between the spouses, for example, can take years to appear. Before this happens, even setbacks can occur with reinforced subordination and subdued self-estimation of the woman. Regardless, significant changes in the status of women in society will depend on a number of other factors, as well, interacting with the labour migration.

The Class Structure

In presenting the empirical data from Colombo and Hambantota I have discussed some of the effects of migration on the individual/household level. I now turn to the added consequences on a higher level of aggregation. As stated, the act of migration may have different consequences on an aggregate level than for the individual and the household. The same act may cause (at least temporarily) socioeconomic mobility for the individual, whereas the community may end up with a new pattern of stratification. The ability to send money home may have a positive impact on a woman's position in the family, although this may not necessarily have changed the status of women as a group nor given them more control over the course of development.

We have hypothesized that female migrants basically are guided by a supporter logic, in the sense that accumulation and expansion are generally out of reach for this group. However, the spending pattern may nevertheless increase the material and social status of the household in the wake of migration (again, at least temporarily). The implicit aspiration is to establish a more secure household basis in terms of daily maintenance as well as a more profound capital base to enable the women to retire from migrant labour. Even though little capital accumulation takes place among members of this group, they may well have established themselves on a somewhat higher social level locally for the time being.

Other groups involved in migration may actually have profited significantly from the migration traffic. First and foremost, this observation applies to the moneylenders. The money market has expanded significantly in the wake of the migration, and the lenders, already with a strong hold on the communities, have been able to utilize this new niche. The extent of big the profits is impossible to trace.

Another group worth mentioning is the local masons. Extensive housebuilding has provided them with a thriving business climate, as it has the trade community in general because more money is circulating. This situation also means, however, that communities of professionals and small-scale traders are vulnerable to changes in the future Middle East migration. I have also mentioned local socioeconomic consequences of migration for the poor without extra income possibilities, who are adversely affected by inflation.

Altogether the stratification picture in sending communities may have changed in the sense that the internal elements may have been reshuffled. On the one hand, it may be that the migrants from the poorer strata climb the ladder a few steps and reduce the distance to the next category. On the other hand, the existence of the two groups—the losers (poor nonmigrants) and the big profiteers (agents and moneylenders)—may make the picture more clearly differentiated.

There is also a possibility that the composition of the housemaid group will change. As agent fees rise, the entry ticket is successively more difficult to obtain. The possibility of borrowing certainly has its limits. There is a threshold beyond which the job is not worth the effort—when the interest on loans approaches the monthly salary overseas. Consequently it will then only be people who can afford the fee with little or no borrowing, or people who can arrange a contract directly, who can afford to go unless the fees are reduced.

As mentioned, education has traditionally had a high standing in the Sri Lankan society, in its own right and as a means to climb the social ladder. One could therefore assume that the Gulf money would be used to increase educational attainment. As we have seen, whereas many migrants state that they would like to spend money on schooling, not many follow up in practice. There could be more reasons for this discrepancy. One is the threshold argument—that they would need much more money than they actually have to invest in order to really count. In other words, they would virtually have to belong to another class to profit from education in a substantial way. Another reason is that migration communities know better than anybody that the easiest access to economic advancement in Sri Lanka today is not primarily through education. Children and their parents may perceive schooling to be dispensable since they observe workers from their own environment, with very little education, earning high incomes abroad. Education has generally been deflated in social value, and the importance of money has gained terrain. The oral commitment by the migrants as to the importance of education could then be attributed to cultural lag in the system. It is nevertheless beyond doubt that a basic education is necessary to get ahead, also in the context of migration. Poor educational standard has been one of the complaints raised by the Gulf states towards the Sri Lankan authorities concerning the maids. This is a growing concern on the Sri Lankan side, since it runs the risk of being out-competed on the market.

I have devoted much space to the role of the class variable and the consequences of female migration in Sri Lanka—the fact that the great majority of these migrants come from poor households. Considering the fairly high level of income of the Middle East migrants compared to that offered for even fairly high-ranking positions among the educated strata in Sri Lanka, it would not be surprising if women from the middle classes should seriously consider the option. The wages might seem so attractive that they would consider spending a couple of years in the Gulf to accumulate some money, since the domestic labour market at present is not particularly favorable to them either.

Compared to the poor women who actually comprise the Sri Lankan contingent, the middle-class women belong to a completely different category in terms of all the resources discussed in relation to the different stages of the migration process. (This is so even though their material basis has deteriorated since the late 1970s, depending on which sector they belonged to.) Different classes provide different contexts for social behaviour. The interlinked resources promoted by birth, language spoken, education, economic basis, network, self-confidence—in short, the resources that to different degrees make them belong to the middle class—would have given these women a starting point far superior to that of poor dwellers of villages or slums. These strong initial resources consequently could have inclined them to handle each link in the migration chain in a more beneficial way. The possibility of an economic uplift should therefore be present to a much greater extent than for the poor.

However, only a very few middle-class women actually go. The reason for this, as already touched on, is mainly cultural or normative, in that doing housework for others is regarded as clearly inferior in Sri Lankan society. This attitude is also reflected in the domestic wage level in this sector. Women with any other alternatives will try to avoid such work. This cultural imperative seems to function even when the work is outside the island and remunerated far above what can be achieved at home. The few lower-middle-class migrating women interviewed in this study underscored the point very clearly. Both the migrants themselves and their families were ashamed of the fact that they were going. In all cases a special reason was given as an explanation: "the husband died" or "an accident ruined the family."

This situation yields something of a paradox. Those who actually go to the Gulf have such a low social position in the first place that they rarely manage to escape from poverty, whereas those who really could give the economy a lift do not utilize the option for other reasons. Instead it becomes urgent for these middle-class women to distance themselves from the mobile maids, who in some cases now can outrank them in having the finest saris and the most gold rings around their arms. Wealth gained through the female Middle East traffic is qualitatively different from the traditional means.

Not surprisingly, better-off women (and men) thus tend to belittle or ridicule these nouveau riche inclinations. Such attitudes are also reflected in newspapers and magazines, where the Middle East women are often shown as figures of fun in cartoons and the like. The condemnation of the Middle East women is often related to middle-class values concerning a woman's duty to stay at home and take care of the family. Representatives of the middle and upper class themselves feel affected by the traffic. Increasingly uneasiness is expressed with the new "Sri Lankan image" internationally: Sri Lanka is gradually being associated with helpless women who travel en masse.

A striking illustration of this class aspect can be found in marriage proposals in different kinds of newspapers in the country. In the local Sunday newspapers being a migrant is often presented as proof of the solvency of the family ("daughter has been twice in Dubai") (Eelens and Schampers, 1986). In the English Sunday newspapers, on the other hand, phrases like "even Mid East Women considered" may occasionally appear.

Generally speaking, the "Dubai women" have slowly made their way into the culture in a broad sense—appearing now in theatre, songs, jokes and cartoons—and predominately in this class biased way.

Macroeconomic Impact

As touched on earlier, it is difficult to find socioeconomic effects that can be attributed to migration alone, without considering other ongoing processes of change. One single socioeconomic phenomenon cannot easily be subject to investigation in isolation. In Sri Lanka this assumption is underscored by the fact that the migration process started and developed at the same time as society was undergoing other major transformations. Central aspects of modernization penetrated the remotest corners of the island almost simultaneously with the first wave of migration. The question of a more complete integration into the capitalist market economy and consequent consumerism cannot therefore be seen as a direct effect of labour migration. The new consumption pattern should rather be viewed as a result of a complex process within the country's political economy, in which labour migration has been an important part since 1980. In this perspective migration can contribute to an acceleration of already existing socioeconomic trends.

The impact of labour migration can be substantially different on different levels of society. As to the individual/household level I have so far concluded that the spending pattern may be economically sensible in terms of the options available under current circumstances. Nevertheless, it does not seem that the traffic to the Middle East will have a lasting constructive impact on the household economy unless the consumption trap can be transcended.

Even though the lasting effects may not be very promising at the microlevel, the scene concerning the local and national economies may be somewhat different. Consumption expenditures, as well as spendings on house construction and durables, are usually considered unproductive, although they may have the potential for raising domestic output through both direct and indirect channels (Arnold, 1988).[9] In particular, using remittances for housing may yield local demand that can generate a multiplier effect in the economy. The housing industry is said typically to have a high ratio of domestic inputs to total inputs (Stahl and Arnold, 1986). It is also probable that activities in the informal sector have been expanding in order to absorb migrants' surplus cash. Moreover, in poor countries spending remittances on education, health and generally better living conditions may contribute to a rise in "human capital," enhancing productivity in the long run.

Remittances from labour migration are often believed to generate higher rates of inflation rather than to increase a country's productive capacities, owing to the special spending priorities of migrants. This result may be the case, although the evidence is somewhat difficult to pursue. One would actually have to follow the remittances through the entire chain of transactions to evaluate the real impact on the economy. The spendings of the migrant household may be significant for the national economy if money that originally was generated in the Middle East is in the end used for productive purposes. However, prices in Sri Lanka have risen significantly during the same period as the labour export has gained momentum. Consumption of imported goods has also increased considerably. Inflationary pressure has also actually affected the value of the remittances. As we saw in the case of Gallegama, later migrants have to work for longer periods abroad to accomplish the same results at home as the pioneer migrants could achieve with one contract.

From a national perspective there are few doubts that labour migration to the Middle East is perceived as an economic investment, particularly in view of the alternative ways of generating foreign exchange. Remittances make it possible for a country to conserve domestic inputs that could otherwise be required for producing goods and services for export to earn foreign exchange. Remittances can therefore be a relatively inexpensive way of generating foreign exchange, provided that the absence of workers does not involve more significant costs (Arnold, 1988).

Another important aspect from the government's point of view is the way remittances can mitigate the rising expectations of the population concerning access to more money and better living conditions. The Middle East money reduces the government's commitment on the social welfare side (Korale, 1983), thus functioning as a social security compensation. The responsibility of improving (or keeping up) standards of living is hence transferred to the family, alleviating the financial burden on the state (Rupesinghe, 1990). The government may also feel it can afford to pay less attention to policies dealing with domestic unemployment.

Whether the net effect is positive for the sender state, however, is subject to much discussion. Although most governments in labour-exporting countries tend to believe in the beneficial sides of migration, there is little empirical evidence of this effect. According to F. Arnold, "for every study which concludes that remittances facilitate economic growth, there is almost always a study that reaches the opposite conclusion. . . . These conclusions often reflect the ideology of the investigator more than unbiased empirical findings" (Arnold, 1988:13; see also Bohning, 1984).

Some of this confusion may be due to the time dimension. Whereas the short-term national effects may in the main be highly beneficial for the reasons mentioned above, the long-term consequences may be more complicated. There are strong indications that having export of labour power as one of the most central elements of the national economy generates dependency[10] unless the remittances are used to diversify the economy in a lasting way. The latter rarely seems to be the case. Sender economies are usually weak, and export of labour is a symptom of this weakness in the sense that a domestic problem is "exported" to get some breathing space. This specific dependency makes the sender economy extremely vulnerable to international fluctuations, both politically and economically (Owen, 1986; Birks and Sinclair, 1980). The Sri Lankan–Middle East case is actually a striking illustration of this outcome, as discussed earlier.

A similar kind of dependency may be created in the sender communities. As long as new economic openings are not generated locally as alternatives to migration, the communities will most likely rely on remittances from the Middle East for daily reproduction. Consequently, even though local trade may experience a temporary surge due to the spin-off effects of remittances, the long-term benefits are uncertain at best. Yet again, studies on the development effect of remittances are extremely difficult to undertake.[11] A serious problem is the general repercussions the new "migrating society" has on the group of poor nonmigrants for whom there is no possibility of profiting by remittances directly or indirectly. Members of this group have found that their earning capacities have been reduced at the same time as their buying capacities are being eroded by inflation.

It is impossible to delineate any uniform total effect of labour migration. As is the case with many socioeconomic phenomena, the individual/household may act according to a different rationale than does the state. Therefore, the sum of individual strategies may not be structurally desirable to national economic planners. People tend to spend their money in fields that yield a rapid, personally favorable result, not paying attention to the long-term interest of the nation. The household is not a capitalist enterprise but rather an entity with value orientation towards consumption and the general well-being of the family. For the majority of the households in question continued subsistence is the basic aim. This reality does not in principle exclude the possibility of growth within this frame. The subsistence scale may move upwards, in the sense that the culturally defined "necessary standard of living" is subject to change. This study concludes that this is actually taking place, at least during the period of migration. People consume more and more expensively but deeper structural changes are not taking place simultaneously. Thus the socioeconomic push—the structural features that generated the migration in the first place—is not basically changed. Lasting alternatives are not created within the national economy, in the sense that production is changed or increased.

The challenge from a strategic perspective would be to make productive investments profitable and realistic for the majority of the migrants. For women migrants this goal is fairly utopian at this point because of the class composition of the working force. In essence, the question is one of coming to grips with the poverty problem of the country.

* * *

The theme of this book has been causes and consequences of female labour migration. The phenomenon has been treated on different levels of abstraction. A central objective has been to show how these different levels with a multitude of elements interact and form the dynamic process that labour migration represents. I have applied a combination of concepts and hypotheses derived from various theoretical traditions. Theories of unequal exchange and international division of labour and, generally, theories of development have been applied on the macrolevel to facilitate an understanding of central mechanisms in motion. On lower levels of abstraction theory of action and particularly gender specific action have been used to grasp the question of motivation behind the move and to explain the particular consequences generated by female migration.

The study has moved from the international context, where flows of labour are seen to move according to economic structures and division of labour among countries at different stages of development, through the national context and down to the individual migrant and her close surroundings.

The trade in labour power has recently become an increasingly important element on the international economic scene. Usually one finds labour moving from countries at lower stages of development to more developed and industrialized areas. Cheap labour power has become a major asset of some developing countries that have pursued an export-oriented development strategy. Export of labour has represented an adjustment to international competition by weaker economies, particularly after the relative decline in prices on raw materials since the 1970s.

This study deals with the way one small country has conquered one of the niches in this landscape—Sri Lanka's comprehensive export of female labour as housemaids to Arab households in the Gulf area. In the field of international labour migration, the traffic to the Gulf is somewhat atypical in one respect: The countries of destination are by and large not highly industrialized or particularly advanced in terms of human capital, their wealth being based on rent appropriation from oil revenues. However, Sri Lanka is a poor developing country despite its resources, and the country competes by having an extremely low wage level as the major attribute.

The macrosection of this study spelled out how coinciding circumstances promoted the migration link between Sri Lanka and the Gulf in the late 1970s. On the one hand, one finds the oil-price boom and the subsequent development programmes cum welfare increase for the population in the Gulf and, on the other, the increased foreign currency need of the new Sri Lankan government and the decline in living standard of the poorer parts of Sri Lanka's population, which make up the female Middle East contingent. This system may be said to constitute a symbiosis although, as in most labour migration contexts, it is indubitably an asymmetrical one.

The microsection dealt with human action in terms of the interplay between motivational factors and structural conditions. I analyzed how this interplay is influenced by concrete facilitators and constraints in society. The combination of these factors will condition both the act of migration itself and the consequences for the woman and her surroundings.

The Motivational Side

The study concludes that the Sri Lankan labour export basically represents an adaptation to grim realities, both for the sender state and for the households involved. It has played a central role in the capitalist economic expansion for the state since 1977, and simultaneously it has been the way in which exploited classes have tried to cope with the financial constraints of their situation. Although the individual women and their households have aspirations as to improving their family's standard of living, we must conclude that it is basically a supporter logic that guides the female migrants rather than any "Grunder mentality" aiming at economic investment and expansion of the economic basis.

This conclusion implies that on the personal side the women rarely reflect any individual striving in relation to migration. The Gulf contract is their contribution to a strained household economy because their labour power is in demand. (This statement does not exclude the possibility that the migrant women may wish to gain some goods for themselves as well, like saris, gold rings and dowry.)

This supporter logic has been variously explained as being class and gender specific. Actually the combination of class and gender explains both the specific composition of the work force and the cumulative results of the process. As to the composition, only women from the lower classes are in such a position that the jobs offered in the Gulf seem attractive. We have seen that this is so for economic, yet even more so for ideological, reasons. Other kinds of better paying jobs abroad are less accessible, as the entrance ticket is more expensive. These jobs are usually covered by men from more well-off groups in society. I have also argued that due to the specific composition of the female workforce to the Gulf and related social characteristics, the outcome of the traffic may be different from that intended.

The Effect Side

Two major assumptions have formed the basis for the study on the effect side: (1) The remittances generated in the Middle

East were believed to give the households involved a significant socioeconomic boost, as salaries of this level are otherwise extremely rare among the poorest sections of Sri Lankan society; (2) some of the extraordinary aspects of the female migration—the drastic shake-up of traditional gender norms in terms of daily male control, geographical mobility and breadwinning—were believed to have some impact on women's emancipation or, rather, reduced subordination.

My conclusions as to the main hypotheses are, however, rather negative in both respects. One must bear in mind the basic qualification of the time dimension—a phenomenon may well have different short- and long-term consequences. We have seen that the major part of the remittances are used for daily household maintenance, meaning that the majority of the sender households need the income from the Middle East to sustain themselves. Often, however, this sustenance is on a higher level than these families had been used to. By and large, the Middle East households eat more and better than the nonmigrating neighbors. Their clothing is also usually better. A fairly large part of the migrating community also manages to improve its housing standard. The supporter logic consequently is relative in the sense that standard of household maintenance is increased.

The massive majority of the migrant households do not, however, manage to escape what we have called the consumption trap, that is, they do not manage to invest in a lasting asset or activity that could promote social progress. The expenditure pattern (usually by necessity) is such that much of the potential benefit for future development is lost. The poor are poor in the kind of resources that could have helped them to pursue some lasting accumulation. Indeed, the cumulative processes work to their detriment all the way through. The result of the initial decision to work abroad becomes structural, in the sense that the causes behind the traffic reproduce themselves. The preconditions for mobility or, rather, securing the economic basis for the household, may not have been there or they may have been undermined during the process. Therefore, if a central motivation of the individual woman or her household was to escape the necessity of going again, the results of the move have been unanticipated.

There are, however, important differences in degree. A major variable when it comes to relative success in handling remittances is whether there are any other stable incomes in the household, an important condition both as a supplementary source of income and as a disciplining factor as to the economic behaviour of the family. Households with a history of stable income, however small, usually have some sense of planning. One conclusion to be drawn is that migration alone will not give a socioeconomic uplift. Other preconditions must be present, as well. The poverty problem intrinsically linked to female migration in Sri Lanka is not solved by migration itself.

Nevertheless, there is a possibility that the social composition of the female contingent may change somewhat in the future because the expenses involved in the traffic seem to be steadily increasing. Whereas the poorest sections so far have had their chance through borrowing money to cover the fees, future options will depend on the relation between salary rate and debt burden.

When it comes to the second main hypothesis—changes in gender structures—the prospects that are spelled out are basically not more optimistic. Because of diverse factors in society that condition and mediate the effects of migration on the position of women, there is no direct answer to the question of whether female migration improves women's status in society and in their homes. Nevertheless, I have discussed some possible connections between the Gulf traffic and gender relations in the households and the sending communities at large.

First and foremost, women's wage work has almost without exception become the major economic asset of the families involved. The female migrants represent the breadwinners of their families at a wage rate that no one in the house has experienced before. In consequence, female labour power, actually and potentially, has become more of an asset to Sri Lankan households. Women's labour has become more visible in society, a factor that will possibly contribute to the changing of the traditional dowry system in the longer run.

Another important consideration when discussing gender effects of female labour migration is the repercussions the traffic has on other female members of the household. As long as the sexual division of labour is clearly defined, in the sense that almost all reproductory work is assigned to women, one woman's possibility implies another woman's burden. We have seen that the eldest daughter or the sister of the migrant often has to sacrifice education or possibly other activities to take care of the "left-behinders."

As we have seen, there are many paradoxes present in this field. It may seem paradoxical that female labour power, otherwise the cheapest available in society, can be sold on the international market to generate salaries that only a few men can achieve in the home market. In fact, the quality of being cheap becomes a valuable asset in a context of heavy unemployment—"the comparative advantage of women's disadvantage" (Charlton, 1981).

The increased involvement of women in the labour market represents principally an improvement of the position of women in Sri Lankan society. It allows them to leave (at least partially) the confines of the home and thereby (temporarily) to stay away from the direct, daily control by the male head of household; it allows them to delay marriage and childbearing if they are not already married or to delay more pregnancies if married; it increases their de facto economic position, and it increases the consumption level of their families.

At the same time the involvement in this international labour market exposes the woman to a new form of exploitation and oppression. The working conditions are often much worse than those she is used to, and her feeling of personal dignity may be basically threatened. We have seen that the money she generates in the Gulf very often slips out of her hands when sent home to the family. In other words, her budget control is rather weak, a fact that underscores her subordinate position. In fact, many husbands seem to reinforce the control of their wives in the wake of migration. We have suggested that this is (at least temporarily) a reaction to their feeling of threatened male identity, of being surpassed by their women in income generation. Lucrative female employment in a context of heavy male unemployment proves not to be a favorable combination. On top of this the domestic work in the Gulf by and large represents a dead-end job for the women involved. The maids start out as unskilled and unexperienced workers, and there are strong indications that they remain unemployed as returnees.

Any conclusions as to the long-term effects of female labour migration from Sri Lanka have to be fairly open-ended as yet. Nevertheless, my main hypothesis is that there are few long-term gains in terms of status, autonomy, fewer burdens or enduring economic security for the women involved based on the assumption that the migrants do not generate any lasting spin-offs in terms of personal employment in their own country.

Quite the opposite, I have hypothesized that this labour migration produces dependence, both for the sender state and for the individuals involved. For the state, migration serves as a breather in the export economy—a safety valve in a situation in which unemployment and lack of foreign currency represent major obstacles to economic growth. Vulnerability and dependency will increase unless economic linkages can be established between migration traffic and internal production, linkages to serve as buffers when migration possibilities are reduced or ended.

For the households concerned we have seen some of the same dependence on a lower level. The poverty syndrome implies that to a great extent migrant households do not manage to create new economic foundations based on women's labour contracts in the Gulf. And so, when the possibilities in the Middle East dry up—either because each household no longer has someone to send or because the recipient countries stop the import—these households will find themselves in a very difficult situation. The housing standard may have improved, as has the health of the children; yet the family income situation is back to square one. Psychologically this reversal will probably even feel worse, since the family has had a foot inside another world and has gotten used to a daily consumption pattern far beyond realistic levels.

All the same, for thousands of Sri Lankan women the "Middle East Avenue" has opened up a new world outside the village and the home. It has broadened their conceptual environment and provided their communities with a more concrete understanding of "abroad." Not least important, the Middle East migration reflects the fact that the women—and their households—become psychologically ready to accept drastic changes in patterns of behaviour when circumstances require it.

Notes

1. The most systematic exception in this respect were the young unmarried Muslim girls, who generally placed the responsibility on their fathers.

2. Radhika Coomaraswamy makes a relevant point in this respect: "It is interesting that when families do become richer and have access to modern technology, household work done by women is the last to be modernized. A cassette player will often precede an electric cooker. In rich Indian peasant homes with TV, cassette-players, and large expensive carpets, the women still cook over a smoky chula or a brick oven stove" (Coomaraswamy, 1984:32).

3. This is also the case in both Westvyke and Alutmahawatha communities where the houses originally were built through a social scheme independent of the Middle East migration but where the subsequent remunerations from abroad were extensively used for further improvements.

4. One should treat this information from the school principals with some reservation, as there often seems to be a moral undertone in the reports, and their own emotional involvement in the issue colors the viewpoints. This could be an example of the "middle-class-resentment" that will be discussed.

5. The concept is derived from Colin Murray (1981), who talks about the "sociology of absenteeism," which has many similar traits.

6. This expression is introduced by Deniz Kandiyoti, although in a slightly different context (Kandiyoti, 1986).

7. See Murray (1981) for an eminent analysis of this phenomenon in the context of Lesotho.

8. These few examples have obviously been quite powerful in forming local opinion, among men in particular, as to the claimed "new assertiveness" of the Middle East maids.

9. In Bangladesh, for example, it is estimated that remittances of $610 million in 1983 produced a final demand of $351 million for Bangladesh goods and services, which would have generated at least 577,000 jobs (Habib, 1985). Similar data on the situation in Sri Lanka are not available.

10. "Dependency" is a rather vague concept, difficult to measure in any precise way. It also tends to be used ideologically. Since any country integrated in the capitalist world economy is "dependent" to a certain degree, one would have to qualify the concept extensively to elaborate on this topic. This is, however, not the aim of this study. Dependence remains a central question in the context of

labour migration when it comes to the long-term perspectives of the phenomenon.

11. One study that has been undertaken in this field does nevertheless conclude that the contribution of the migration to village development has been negligible and that "the main impact of migration appears to be largely confined to improving the living standards of the emigrant families rather than restructuring the production potential of the communities" (Dias,1983).

References

Abadan-Unat, Nermin, 1986: "International labour migration and its effect upon women's occupational and family roles: A Turkish view," in UNESCO, 1986.

Abello, Manolo I., 1984: "Labour migration from South and South-East Asia: Some policy issues," *International Labour Review,* 123 (4).

Afshar, Haleh, 1985: "Introduction," in Haleh Afshar (ed.), *Women, work, and ideology in the third world,* London, Tavistock.

Akinci, A. Ugur, 1982: "Differentiation of capital and international labour migration: Constructing a working hypothesis," *International Migration Review,* 20 (1/2).

Amin, S. (ed.), 1974: "Introduction," in *Modern migrations in Western Africa,* London, Oxford University Press.

Amin, S., 1976: *Unequal development: An essay in the social formation of peripheral capitalism.* London, Harvester.

Arnold, Fred, 1988: "The contribution of remittances to economic and social development," paper presented at a seminar on International Migration Systems, Processes and Policies, Malaysia, September.

Arnold, Fred, and Nasra M. Shah (eds.), 1986: *Asian labor migration: Pipeline to the Middle East,* Boulder, Westview.

Bach, Robert L., and Lisa A. Schraml, 1982: "Migration, crisis and theoretical conflict," *International Migration Review,* 16 (2).

Beneria, Lourdes, 1982: "Accounting for women's work," in L. Beneria (ed.), *Women and development: The sexual division of labour in rural societies,* New York, Praeger.

Berger, Peter L., and Thomas Luckmann, 1979: *Den samfundsskabte virkelighet,* Copenhagen, Lindhardt og Ringhof.

Birks, J. S., and C. A. Sinclair, 1980: *International migration and development in the Arab region,* Geneva, International Labour Organization.

Bohning, W. R., 1984: *Studies in international labour migration,* London, Macmillan.

Bonacich, Edna, and Lucie Cheng, 1984: *Labour immigration under capitalism: Asian workers in the United States before World War II,* Berkely, University of California Press.

Bradby, B., 1982: "The remystification of value," *Capital and Class,* 17, Summer.

Cardona, R., and A. Simmons, 1975: "Towards a model of migration in Latin America," in B. M. du Toit and H. I. Safa, (eds.), *Migration and urbanization,* The Hague, Mouton.

Census of Population, 1981, Department of Census and Statistics, Colombo.

Census of Population and Housing, 1971 and 1981, Department of Census and Statistics, Colombo.

Central Bank of Ceylon, 1973: "The determinants of labour force participation rates in Sri Lanka," Colombo.

CENWOR, 1985: *The UN decade for women: Progress and achievements of women in Sri Lanka,* Sridevi, Colombo.

Chapman, Murray, and R. M. Prothero, 1983: "Themes on circulation in the third world," *International Migration Review,* 17 (4).

Charlton, Sue E.M., 1981: *Women in the third world development,* London, Westview.

Cliffe, L., 1978: "Labour migration and peasant differentiation," *Journal of Peasant Studies,* 5 (3).

Coomaraswamy, Radhika, 1984: "A working paper on ethnicity and patriarchy," International Centre for Ethnic Studies (ICES), Colombo, September.

De Jong, F. Gordon, and James Fawcett, 1981: "Motivations for migration: An assessment and a value-expectancy research model," in F. Gordon De Jong and Robert W. Gardner (eds.), *Migration decision making: Multidisciplinary approaches to microlevel studies in developed and developing countries,* New York, Pergamon.

Demery, L., 1986: "Asian labor migration: An empirical assessment," in Arnold and Shah, 1986.

De Silva, K. M., 1981: *A history of Sri Lanka,* Los Angeles, University of California Press.

Dias, Malsiri, 1985: "Participation of women in community action," in CENWOR, 1985.

Dias, Malsiri, 1983: "Migration to the Middle East: Sri Lanka case study," Report to UNESCO, Colombo.

Economic Review, 1985: Colombo, June.

Edholm, F. O. Harris, and K. Young, 1977: "Conceptualizing women," *Critique of Anthropology,* 3 (9/10).

Eelens, F., and T. Schampers, 1986: "The effect of migration on the well-being of Sri Lankan children left behind," paper presented at the Workshop on Foreign Employment, Marga Institute.

Eelens, Frank, and Toon Schampers, 1986: "The process of labour migration from Sri Lanka to the Middle East," paper presented at the Seventeenth Summer Seminar in Population, East West Centre, Honolulu.

Eelens, F., and T. Schampers, 1988: "Sri Lankan housemaids in the Middle East," paper presented at the Conference on Women's Position and Demographic Change in the Course of Development, Oslo.

Eelens, F., T. Schampers, and J. D. Speckmann (eds.), 1992: *Labour migration to the Middle East: A case study of Sri Lanka,* London, Kegan Paul International.

Elster, Jon, 1979: *Forklaring og dialektikk,* Oslo, Pax.

Fladby, Berit, 1983: "Household viability and economic differentiation in Gama, Sri Lanka," Bergen Occasional Papers in Social Anthropology, no. 28, Bergen, Department of Social Anthropology.

Fladby, Berit, 1983b: "Kvinnens stilling i et singalesisk bondesamfunn: Arbeidsdeling og sosial status," paper presented at the University of Troms, November.

Foster-Carter, A., 1978: "The modes of production controversy," *New Left Review,* no. 107.

Foucault, Michel, 1983: "Why study power: The question of the subject," in Hubert C. Dreyfus and Paul Robinow, *Beyond structuralism and hermeneutics: Michel Foucault,* Chicago, University of Chicago Press.

Franklin, Rob, 1985: "Migrant labour and the politics of development in Bahrain," *Merip Reports,* May.

Gerold-Scheepers, T.J.F.A., and W.M.J. van Binsberger, 1978: "Marxist and non-Marxist approaches to migration in tropical Africa," in van Binsberger and Meilink, 1978.

Goldstein, S., 1976: "Facets of redistribution: Research challenges and opportunities," *Demography,* 13.

Goonatilake, Hema, 1985: "Women and the media," in CENWOR, 1985.

Goonesekere, Savitri, 1985: "The impact of the UN Decade for Women on the legal status of Sri Lankan women," in CENWOR, 1985.

Gunder Frank, A., 1971: *Capitalism and underdevelopment in Latin America,* London, Penguin.

Guyer, J. I., and P. E. Peters, 1987: "Conceptualizing the household: Issues of theory and policy in Africa," *Development and Change,* 18 (2).

Habib, A., 1985: *Economic consequences of international migration for sending countries: Review of evidence from Bangla Desh,* Newcastle, Australia, University of Newcastle.

Halliday, Fred, 1984: "Labour migration in the Arab world," *Merip Reports,* May.

Harris, Olivia, 1981: *Households as natural units,* in Young et al., 1981.

Harris, Olivia, and Kate Young, 1981: "Engendered structures: Some problems in the analysis of reproduction," in J. Llobera and J. Kahn (eds.), *The anthropology of pre-capitalist societies,* London, Macmillan.

Harris, J. R., and M. Todaro, 1970: "Migration, unemployment and development: A two sector analysis," *American Economic Review,* 60, March.

Heyzer, Noeleen, 1981: "Towards a framework of analysis," in Moser and Young, 1981.

Heyzer, Noeleen (ed.), 1985: *Missing Women: Development planning in Asia and the Pacific,* Kuala Lumpur, Asian and Pacific Development Centre.

Heyzer, Noeleen, 1986: *Working women in South-East Asia: Development, subordination and emancipation,* Philadelphia, Open University Press.

Hugo, Graeme J., 1981: "Village-community ties, village norms and ethnic and social networks: A review of evidence from the third world," in F. Gordon De Jong and Robert Gardner (eds), *Migration decisionmaking: Multidisciplinary approaches to microlevel studies in developed and developing countries,* New York, Pergamon.

Jayawardene, Kumari, 1985: "Some aspects of feminist consciousness in the decade 1975–1985," in CENWOR, 1985.

Jayawardene, Kumari, and Swarna Jayaweera, 1985: "The integration of women in development planning: Sri Lanka," in Heyzer, 1985.

Jayaweera, Swarna, 1979: "Women and education," in University of Colombo, 1979.

Jayaweera, Swarna, 1984: *Women in the context of ethnicity, law and social reality: The Sri Lankan case,* International Center for Ethnic Studies (ICES), September.

Jayaweera, Swarna, 1985: "Women and education," in CENWOR, 1985.

Jørgensen, Kirsten, and Mette Mønsted (eds.), 1983: *U-lands-kvinner i landbruget,* København, Kvindernes U-landsudvalg.

Kandiyoti, Deniz, 1986: *Deconstructing patriarchy,* paper presented at the International Peace Research Institute of Oslo (PRIO), Oslo, April.

Kandiyoti, Deniz, 1988: *Women and rural development policies: The changing agenda,* IDS Discussion Paper, no. 44, May.

Kerven, C., 1980: *Botswana mine labour migration to South Africa,* National Migration Study issue paper no. 3, Rural Sociology Unit, Ministry of Agriculture, Botswana.

Korale, R.B.M., 1983: "Migration for employment to the Middle East: Its demographic and socio-economic effects on Sri Lanka," paper, Colombo.

Korale, R.B.M., et al., 1985: *Foreign employment: Sri Lanka experience,* Colombo, Ministry of Plan Implementation.

Korale, R.B.M., 1985b: *Middle East migration: The Sri Lankan experience,* in Asian Population Studies Series no. 64, International Migration in the Pacific, Sri Lanka and Thailand, United Nations, Bankok.

Kuhn, A., and A. M. Wolpe, 1978: *Feminism and materialism. Women and modes of production,* Boston, Routledge and Kegan Paul.

Lee, E. S., 1966, "A theory of migration," *Demography,* 3 (1).

Lewis, W. A., 1954: "Economic development with unlimited supplies of labour," Manchester School of Economic and Social Studies, 22, May.

Liljestrom, Rita, 1983: *Fruktsamhetsreglering på Sri Lanka,* Stockholm, SIDA.

Lim, Linda, 1983: "Capitalism, imperialism and patriarchy: The dilemma of third world women workers in multinational factories," in June Nash, et al. (eds.), *Women, men and the international division of labour,* New York, State University of New York Press.

Longva, A. N., 1990: "Power, dependence and cultural dilemmas: The presence of migrant workers in Kuwait and its repercussions on the local society," unpublished paper.

Mackintosh, Maureen, 1981: "The sexual division of labour and the subordination of women," in Young et al., 1981.

Marga Institute, 1986: "Migrant workers to the Arab world," Institute publication, Colombo.

Marx, Karl, 1867: *Capital,* vol. 1, London, Lawrence and Wishart, 1970.

Meilink, H. A., 1978: *Migration and the transformation of modern African society: Introduction, African Perspective,* no. 1.

Meillassoux, C., 1975: *Maidens, meal and money: Capitalism and the domestic community,* London, Cambridge University Press.

Mies, Maria, 1986: *Patriarchy and accumulation on a world scale,* London, Zed.

Molyneux, Maxine, 1979: "Beyond the domestic labour debate," *New Left Review,* no. 116.

Mook, Tineke, 1992: "Selectivity and access to migration opportunities for women to the Middle East: A village case study," in Eelens, Schampers and Speckmann, 1991.

Moore, Mick, 1985: *The state and peasant politics in Sri Lanka,* London, Cambridge University Press.

Morokvasic, Mirjana, 1984: "Migrant women in Europe: A comparative perspective," in UNESCO, 1986.

Moser, Caroline, 1981: *Surviving in the suburbios,* in IDS Bulletin, 12 (3).

Moser, Caroline, and Kate Young, 1981: *Women of the working poor,* IDS Bulletin, 12 (3).

Murray, Colin, 1981: *Families divided: The impact of migrant labour in Lesotho,* London, Cambridge University Press.

Myrdal, G., 1957: *Economic theory and underdeveloped regions,* London, Duckworth.

Nagi, Mostafa H., 1986: "Determinants of current trends and the future outlook," in Arnold and Shah, 1986.

Nikolinakos, Marios, 1976: "Notes towards a general theory of migration," *Economic Review,* February.

Owen, Roger, 1986: *Migrant workers in the Gulf,* Minority Rights Group, Report no. 68, London.

Penninx, Rinus, 1986: "Theories on international labour migration: between micro and macro analysis," paper presented at the Eleventh World Congress of Sociology, New Delhi, August.

Portes, Alejandro, and John Walton, 1981: *Labour class and the international system,* New York, Academic Press.

Postel, Els, and Joke Schrijvers (eds.), 1980: *A woman's mind is longer than a kitchen spoon: Report on women in Sri Lanka,* research project Women and Development, Colombo-Leiden, Rijksuniversiteit, Leiden, June.

Pryor, Robin J., 1975: "The motivation of migration: A causal nexus," in R. Pryor (ed.), *The motivation of migration,* Canberra, Australian National University.

Ravenstein, E. G., 1885: "The laws of migration," *Journal of the Royal Statistical Society,* 52, June.

Redclift, Nanneke, 1985: "The contested domain: Gender, accumulation and the labour process," in Redclift and Mingione.

Redclift, N., and E. Mingione (eds.), 1985: *Beyond employment: Household, gender and subsistence,* Oxford, Basil Blackwell.

Richards, Alan, and Philip L. Martin, 1983: "The laissez-faire approach to international labour migration: The case of the Arab Middle East," in *Economic Development and Cultural Change,* 31 (3).

Rogers, Barbara, 1980: *The domestication of women: Discrimination in developing countries,* London.

Rupesinghe, Kumar, 1990: *The social and economic conditions of export oriented industrialization as a strategy of development,* Hong Kong, Arena.

Sanderatne, Nimal, 1985: "The effects of policies on real income and employment," in Unicef, 1985.

Sarath, U. G., 1984: "Middle East migration and its impact on the economy of Sri Lanka," University of Colombo, September.

Sherbiny, Naiem, 1984: "Expatriate labour flows to the Arab oil countries in the 1980's," *Middle East Journal,* 38 (4).

Sørbø, Gunnar, et al., 1987: *Sri Lanka: Country study and Norwegian aid,* University of Bergen, Centre for Development Studies.

Spaan, Ernst, 1992: "Socio-economic conditions of Sri Lankan migrant workers in the Gulf states," in Eelens, Schampers and Speckmann, 1992.

Stahl, C. W., and Fred Arnold, 1986: "Overseas workers' remittances in Asian development," *International Migration Review,* 20 (4).

Standing, Guy, 1985: "Circulation and the labour process," in G. Standing (ed.), *Labour circulation and the labour process,* London, Croom Helm.

Taylor, J. G., 1979: *From modernization to modes of production: A critique of the sociologies of development and underdevelopment,* London, Macmillan.

Tienda, Marta, and Karen Booth, 1988: "Migration, gender and social change: A review and reformulation," in International Union for the Scientific Study of Population (IUSSP), Conference on women's position and demographic change in the course of development, Oslo.

Unicef, 1985: *Sri Lanka: The social impact of economic policies during the last decade,* Colombo.

UNESCO, 1986: "Women on the move: Contemporary changes in family and society," Paris.

University of Colombo, 1979: "Status of women, Sri Lanka," in CENWOR 1985.

van Binsberger, W.M.J., and H. A. Meilink, 1978: "Migration and the transformation of modern African society: Introduction," *African Perspective,* no. 1.

Voice of Women, 1982: "Sri Lankan housemaids in the Middle East," *Voice of Women, Sri Lankan Journal of Women's Emancipation,* no. 4, July.

Wallerstein, Immanuel, 1974: "The modern world system: Capitalist agriculture and the origins of the European world economy in the sixteenth century," New York, Academic Press.

Warren, Bill, 1973: "Imperialism and capitalist industrialization," *New Left Review,* no. 81.

Wolpe, H. (ed.), 1980: *The articulation of modes of production: Essays from* Economy and Society, London, Routledge and Kegan Paul.

Women's Bureau, 1981: *Study of female migrant workers to the Middle East,* Colombo.

Wood, Charles H., 1982: "Equilibrium and historical-structural perspectives on migration," *International Migration Review,* 16 (2).

York Smith, Michael, 1986: "Hambantota District, Sri Lanka," in *Integrated Rural Development Programme, 1979–1985: A Description,* NORAD, Colombo.

Young, Kate, 1978: "Modes of appropriation and the sexual division of labour: A case study from Oaxaca, Mexico," in Kuhn and Wolpe, 1978.

Young, K., Carol Wolkowitz, and Roslyn McCullagh, 1981: *Of marriage and the market: Women's subordination in international perspective,* London, CSE.

Zahlan, Antoine B., 1984: "Migratory labour in the Arab world," *Third World Quarterly,* 6 (4).

About the Book and Author

Contributing to the literature on labor migration from less developed countries to the Gulf states, this sociological analysis focuses on the case of Sri Lanka's large-scale exportation of its poorest women to serve as housemaids in private Arab homes. Dr. Brochmann provides a multileveled examination of the social structures that precondition the migration. Considering the household, the village, and Sri Lanka in the world economy, *Middle East Avenue* probes the causes of this traffic and its effects on the economy, society, and gender relations of the participants.

Grete Brochmann is senior researcher at the Institute for Social Research in Oslo.

Index